LIFE AND DOCTRINE

OF

SAINT CATHERINE
OF GENOA

Including

SPIRITUAL DIALOGUE BETWEEN THE SOUL, THE BODY,
SELF-LOVE, THE SPIRIT, HUMANITY, AND THE LORD GOD

and

TREATISE ON PURGATORY

Front cover: From: *Saint Catherine of Genoa* by Domenico
                Piola, engraved by Bartolomeo Giuseppe
                Tasnière.

Title page: From a contemporary portrait of Catherine,
                attributed to her cousin, Tomasina Fieschi.

ISBN: 978-1-78139-221-8

Printed on acid free ANSI archival quality paper.

Contents

Introduction..1

LIFE AND DOCTRINE OF SAINT CATHERINE OF GENOA 9

Chapter I *Of the parents and ancestors of the blessed Catherine, and how at eight years of age she began to do penance; her gift of prayer, and of her desire to enter into religion, and her marriage against her will.* 9

Chapter II *She is wounded with divine love in the presence of her confessor. Manifestations of the love of God and of her own offences. The Lord appears to her carrying his cross, and she is taken up three degrees toward God.* 12

Chapter III *How the desire was given her to receive holy communion, and of its precious effects in her; of her sufferings when she did not receive, and how it seemed to her that she had lost faith, and walked by sight.* 16

Chapter IV *How she was unable to take food during Lent and Advent, being sustained by the Blessed Sacrament* 19

Chapter V *Of her great penances and mortifications* 21

Chapter VI *How she was withdrawn by God from the use of her senses. Of three rules given her by the Lord, and of certain words chosen from the Our Father and Hail Mary, and from the whole of the Holy Scripture.* 23

Chapter VII *How even her humanity was affected by the burning fire of this love; how much she desired to die, and took delight in hearing masses, bells, and offices, for the dead.* 25

Chapter VIII *How the Saint devoted herself to pious works, and served in a hospital.* 28

Chapter IX *Of her wonderful knowledge of God and of herself.* ...30

Chapter X *How impossible it was for vain-glory to enter the mind of this holy creature. Of the light which hatred of self gave her, and of the value of our own actions.* 33

Chapter XI *Of the revelation she had concerning purity of conscience, and of the opposition of sin to God.* 34

Chapter XII *Of the great and solicitous care which God operates in divers ways in order to attract the soul to himself, so that he seems to be in a manner our servant.—Of the blindness of man.—Of the many ways in which he is deceived by his own self-will.* 37

Chapter XIII *How she sees the source of goodness is in God, and how creatures participate in it.* 40

Chapter XIV *How she was entirely transformed in God, and hated to say me or mine.—What pride is.—Of the error of man who seeks for plenty and happiness on earth, where they cannot be found.—What a misfortune it is to be without love.* 43

Chapter XV *How contrary to pure love is even the slightest imperfection.—Of the many means by which God ministers to our salvation.—At the point of death we shall esteem the opposition made to the divine inspirations as worse than hell itself.* 48

Chapter XVI *That she understood her own nothingness, and therefore would not speak about herself.—Of her great faith in God.—How willful and malicious we are in ourselves, and how necessary it is to abandon all to God.* 51

Chapter XVII *In what manner God deals with one who corresponds with him.—And how the saint abhorred spiritual delights, and how God cast around her the chain of pure love.* 56

Chapter XVIII *How she did not desire love for God or in God, nor to have any medium between herself and God.—She could not see how love could be increased in her.—Of the peace of the soul transformed in God.* 59

Chapter XIX *Of her earnest answer to a Friar Preacher who told her how much better he was prepared than herself for the divine love.—Nothing can hinder divine love, neither can it be deceived.—Also of its various conditions.* 62

Chapter XX *That God does not wish man to serve him through self-interest or through fear, but only through faith and love, and therefore he sweetly attracts his will.—The saint did not desire grace or mercy, but only justice.—That pure love fears nothing but sin.* 65

Chapter XXI *How she was disposed toward God and toward her neighbor.—What pure and simple love is.* 70

Chapter XXII *Of her vocation, which was like that of St. Paul.— That she was freed from suffering by her great love.—How terrible is man without grace.—How great is the stain of even one slight defect, and still more that of a sin.* 72

Chapter XXIII *Of self-love and of divine love, and of their conditions.* 76

Chapter XXIV *Concerning the three ways which God takes to purify the creature.* 80

Chapter XXV *The manner in which the saint was medically treated for bodily infirmity, when her suffering was from spiritual fire, and of other accidents that befell her.* 82

Chapter XXVI *Of the three things to which she could not consent, and of those which she could not refrain from desiring.* 84

Chapter XXVII *Of the sweetness of the divine precepts, and the advantage of temporal adversity.* 86

Chapter XXVIII *The process of annihilation of man in God illustrated by the figure of the eating of bread.—Of her interior and exterior.* 88

Chapter XXIX *The saint urged to give an idea of her state.* 89

Chapter XXX *Of her compunction for having desired death, every desire being an imperfection.—She relates her conversion to one of her spiritual children.* 91

Chapter XXXI *How the saint left the whole care of herself to Love; and what means Love employed to purify her from her imperfections.* 93

Chapter XXXII *How well regulated was the saint in all things.—Of the opposition of her spirit to humanity, and how humanity tormented her.* 95

3

Chapter XXXIII *How an evil spirit, that had possession of one of her spiritual daughters, named her Catherine Serafina.* 98

Chapter XXXIV *How the Saint gained a spiritual director.* 100

Chapter XXXV *Treatment of the saint by her husband, and how she obtained salvation of his soul from God, and also that of Sister Tommasa Fiesca, her companion.* 104

Chapter XXXVI *How a person, hopelessly ill, was cured by the prayers of the saint.* 107

Chapter XXXVII *Continuing an account of her extraordinary way of life, and her wonderful condition for some time before her death.* 110

Chapter XXXVIII *How the sufferings she was to endure were revealed to her in spirit; and how dreadful they were to her humanity.—Seeing an image of the woman of Samaria, she asked of God that water.—Of a difference that arose between the spirit and humanity, and of other wonderful things.* 112

Chapter XXXIX *How the spirit deprived her of her confessor, who concealed himself where he could witness her peace of mind in the midst of these tortures.—She had visions of angels.—Of the experiments tried by various physicians.—Of one who had come from England.—Of further divine operations.* 115

Chapter XL *Of the many visions which the saint beheld in her last days.—Of her acute sufferings.—How she could taste nothing but the blessed sacrament, and suffered in herself the pains of the passion of our Lord.* 119

Chapter XLI *In what manner, and at what time, she passed from this life to the Lord.—Many persons saw that blessed soul, under different forms, and in different ways, unite itself with God.—What happened to her confessor when he was celebrating the Mass of the Martyrs.* 124

Chapter XLII *Of her burial, and how the body was preserved in the midst of great moisture and putrefaction.—How many prayers were granted by her intercession, and a person restored to health.—Of the order she gave to have her heart opened, which was not done.* 127

SPIRITUAL DIALOGUE BETWEEN THE SOUL, THE BODY, SELF-
LOVE, THE SPIRIT, HUMANITY, AND THE LORD GOD 129

FIRST PART 131

Chapter I *The soul and the body propose to travel in company, and
to take self-love for a third party.* 131

Chapter II *The Soul and the Body take their turns, in which each
enjoys itself according to its wishes and tastes.* 134

Chapter III *How Self-Love blames both the Soul and the Body, and
wishes to rule them himself.—The Soul complains, and the
Body, adhering to Self-Love, demands what its needs require.*
....136

Chapter IV *The Soul, the Body, and Self-Love pursue their journey,
during which the Soul cannot complete her whole week, and the
Body encroaches upon it.—The Soul allows herself to be
persuaded by Self-Love under pretext of the necessities of her
two companions.—The Soul laments her condition and
proposes not to take her turn again.* 139

Chapter V *The Soul yields to the allurements of the Body and of
Self-Love, and falls into the depths of sin.—Of the little
satisfaction she takes in earthly things, and the trifles that are
sufficient to content the Body.—Of the troubles of the Soul.* ...141

Chapter VI *How the Soul discourses further with Self-Love,
proposing a new mode of action.—Of the nature of Self-Love.—
Of the little required to satisfy the desires of the Body.—How
the Soul falls into misery and despair.* 145

Chapter VII *Of the light which God gave to the Soul to discover all
her faults, and the state into which she had sunk.—Of her
submission, confidence, and conversion.* 149

Chapter VIII *Of many illuminations received by the Soul, and of
the pure love of God.—Of conscience, and the remorse which
God awakens in it.* 151

Chapter IX *The Soul speaks to Self-Love and the Body of the truth
she had seen, and tells them that she should be lost if she
followed them.—She warns them of her purpose to do to them
what they had designed to do to her, namely, to subject them to
herself.—Of the disgust they felt at this.* 156

5

Chapter X *Of the view which the Soul has of the goodness and providence of God.—Of her faults and imperfections.—Of her esteem of herself and hatred of her Humanity.* 160

Chapter XI *How the Soul turns to God and perceives her own sinfulness, and also what she would have become had she continued her former course.—Almost in despair she bewails her offences.—Of the confidence with which our Lord inspires her, appearing to her spirit; and of the wound she receives..* 162

Chapter XII *How God once more manifested to the Soul the love with which he had suffered for her.—She sees the malice of man and the pure love of God.—Of the offering, which she makes of herself to God, and of the wound she receives.—Of the five fountains of Jesus.—Of his constant and jealous watchfulness.* 165

Chapter XIII *Of the instinct which led her to cast off every superfluous thing, and even that appear necessary.—Of her instinct for prayer and her mortification.* 168

Chapter XIV *Of the words that passed between the Spirit and Humanity.—Of the complaints made by Humanity against the fervor of the Spirit which she thought she could endure no longer.* 170

Chapter XV *Humanity complains that the Spirit does not keep its promises and the Spirit defends itself against this charge.—Of the perils of spiritual delights under the semblance of good, and how they are more dangerous than bodily pleasures, which are evidently contrary to the Spirit.—Of the threats of the Spirit against its Humanity.* 172

Chapter XVI *Humanity prays the Spirit to act justly and with equity, reminding her that she had been the first to sin and that the body had been merely the instrument.—The Spirit proves the contrary, and shows who has been the cause of their fall.—The Spirit demonstrates also the necessity of purification here, and that it is better to suffer for a thousand years in this world than one hour in purgatory.* 175

Chapter XVII *God pours into and diffuses throughout the soul a divine sweetness, whereat she complains, not desiring any proof of love.—God, notwithstanding, leaves her plunged in a sea of divine love.—He gives her, also, a vision of pure Love, and another of Self-Love and of her own evil inclinations.* 178

Chapter XVIII *Humanity laments and asks for something to do.— The Spirit consents and enjoins upon it that it should be obedient to all things, stopping at nothing for any pleasure or displeasure that it might feel therein.—Of the rules he wishes to observe; and of the prohibition he imposes upon it of forming no particular friendships.* 180

Chapter XIX *Of the poverty in which the Spirit compelled Humanity to live.—How she was obliged to visit the poor and sick.—Of the suffering she found among them.—Of the oppression and interior distress which she experienced.* 182

Chapter XX *Humanity having tried both exterior suffering and interior distress, the Spirit allows her to choose between them.* 184

Chapter XXI *The Spirit brings Humanity to consent to take up her abode in a hospital, where she served the sick in the humblest manner, doing everything that she was ordered to do.—When she became accustomed to whatever she naturally most abhorred, she was made directress of the hospital, and was gifted with the prudence necessary for this office.—How the burning flame of love ever increased within her.* 186

SPIRITUAL DIALOGUES PART SECOND 189

Chapter I *Of a new love which God poured into her heart, by which he drew her Spirit to himself.—The Soul follows it, so that her powers are absorbed and lost in this love, and the Body, being subject to the Soul, becomes bewildered and changed from its natural condition.* 189

Chapter II *In what manner God keeps the Soul occupied in his love.—Of the weakness of the body and of the support it receives from creatures.—Of the extreme sufferings of Humanity, which it bemoans without complaining, being interiorly conformed to the will of God.—And how purgatory in this life is severe and sweet and full of mercy.* 192

Chapter III *Humanity, thus menaced, desires to know the cause.— This is promised her.—God, while seeking men, draws them by different means and inspirations.—Of her continual sorrow.*

7

How, in her affliction, she calls upon God to relieve her by one ray of his love.—When she comes to understand the grace God has given her, she is pierced by a new dart of love.—Of her confession and contrition. 195

Chapter IV *God sends into that heart another ray of love, which, diffusing itself, fills the soul and revives the body.—There is nothing but exceeding love and joy, until this love, which is wholly from God, has completed its work.* 197

Chapter V *The Soul asks concerning this love.—Our Lord in part answers her and discourses to her upon its greatness, nature, properties, causes and effects.* 199

Chapter VI *God reveals to the Soul that the body is to be purgatory for her in this world.—How necessary it is that man should deny himself and become wholly lost in God.—Of the misery of man when he occupies himself with aught beside, since he has no time but the present to acquire a treasure of merit.* 201

Chapter VII *The Soul, confirmed in virtue, begins to rest in her Lord.—God permits her to see that loving operations whereby, through his great goodness alone, he had liberated her.—The Soul, perceiving her own miseries, burns with a continual flame and is unable to speak or thing of aught besides.* 203

Chapter VIII *Our Lord makes known to the Soul that she had merited nothing, having employed in purifying herself the time which was given her to increase in grace and glory.—Also he shows her that without his help she could have done nothing.* 205

Chapter IX *The Spirit, seeing the Soul brought to the gates of divine love, resolves to subject both Soul and Body to severe suffering.—He tells the Soul that he will separate himself from her, and that in order to recover her first purity, she must pass through many trials.* 207

Chapter X *The Soul discovers that she must make satisfaction voluntarily, and it seems to her that she is abandoned by God.—She calls upon others for help.—How Humanity, by whom she had been threatened, is put to the proof.—Of the sufferings of the Body when deprived of communications with the Spirit.* 210

Chapter XI *Of the brightness of eternal glory, and of the strength imparted to Humanity by a glimpse of it.—How God draws the Spirit to himself, so that it may be wholly occupied in him.—Of its sufferings.—What it is to live on earth while the Spirit is in heaven, and through what sufferings one must pass in order to escape purgatory.* 213

SPIRITUAL DIALOGUES PART THIRD 217

Chapter I *The Soul inquires of God the reason of his great love for man, who is so opposed to him; and also what is man, for whom he cares so much.* 217

Chapter II *Exclamations of the Soul.—Our Lord demands the cause of her surprise, and questions her concerning her enjoyment in the company of spiritual persons, and of the pleasing conversations held with them.* 221

Chapter III *The Soul discovers that what she had been doing, as if for God, proceeded truly from Self-Love.—She is filled with astonishment at the sight of pure love, and inquires concerning its nature.—Our Lord answers her that she could not understand it, and that he himself, being love, can be comprehended only in his effects.* 223

Chapter IV *That he whose heart is pure knows the love of God.—How that love works secretly, subtly, and without exterior occupation.—Some of its effects.—Exclamations of the Soul upon this love.—Of its properties.* 226

Chapter V *Other effects of love.—What it accomplishes at its will.—The work is all its own.—Of works wrought through love, in love, and by love, with some explanation of them.* 230

Chapter VI *The Soul asks various questions of our Lord.—What the martyrs have suffered for this love.—That charity is the shortest and most secure road to salvation, and that without it the Soul would rather cast itself into a thousand hells than enter the presence of God.* 234

Chapter VII *Our Lord questions the Soul concerning the love she feels and on what he has said to her.—The Soul responds according to her ability, but cannot express the intensity of her love.—She asks our Lord how the loving Soul can live on earth, and concerning her condition.* 236

Chapter VIII *Of the condition of the loving Soul.—How God delays imparting to her the knowledge of her defects, since she could not endure it.—She has no repose so long as she suspects the existence of any fault by which her Spirit is hindered of its satisfaction.* 239

Chapter IX *Of the condition of the Body, and in what suffering Humanity found itself, living as though dead.—How God provided for it.—Of the joy experienced by the Soul in the interchange of love, and how she is left like one dead when deprived of it.* 242

Chapter X *How the Soul, the heart, and the Spirit of this creature are devoid of form, and employed in an occupation which cannot be known by their means.—That the heart becomes the tabernacle of God, into which he infuses many graces and consolations, which produce admirable fruits.—That few creatures are led by this road.—Of the nudity of the Spirit and of its union with God.* 245

Chapter XI *Of the secret means used by God for the purification of man.—Of the loving care he takes of him.—How he sweetly leads him by love, and does not allow him to work for his own advantage.—That true nakedness of spirit cannot be expressed by words.* 248

Chapter XII *Exclamations of the Soul upon the blindness which creatures offer to the love of God.—Of the secret operations of God in man, arousing and admonishing him with love.—The Soul inquires concerning this work, and desires to know what grace is, and what is the ray of love.* 250

Chapter XIII *That love cannot be comprehended, and that the heart filled with it lives content.—Of the great mercy which God shows man in this life.—That his justice becomes apparent at the moment when the Soul leaves the body and passes to its destined place.—That the Soul can find repose in God only.* 253

TREATISE ON PURGATORY 257

Chapter I *The state of souls in purgatory.—They are exempt from all self-love.* 257

Chapter II *The joy of souls in purgatory.—The saint illustrates their ever increasing vision of God.—The difficulty of speaking about their state.* 259

Chapter III *Separation from God is the greatest pain of purgatory.—In this, purgatory differs from hell.* 261

Chapter IV *The difference between the state of the souls in hell and that of those in purgatory.—Reflections of the saint upon those who neglect their salvation.* 263

Chapter V *Of the peace and joy which are found in purgatory* ...265

Chapter VI *A comparison to express with how great violence of love the souls in purgatory desire to enjoy God.* 266

Chapter VII *Of the marvelous wisdom of God in the creation of purgatory and of hell.* 267

Chapter VIII *Of the necessity of purgatory, and of its terrific character* 268

Chapter IX *How God and the soul reciprocally regard each other in purgatory.—The saint confesses that she has no words to express these things.* 269

Chapter X *How God makes use of purgatory to complete the purification of the soul.—That she acquires therein a purity so great that if she were yet to remain after her purification she would cease to suffer.* 271

Chapter XI *The desire of souls in purgatory to be purified from every stain of sin.—The wisdom of God in veiling from them their defects.* 272

Chapter XII *How joy and suffering are united in purgatory* 273

Chapter XIII *The souls in purgatory are not in a state to merit.— How they regard the suffrages offered for them in this world.* 274

Chapter XIV *Of the submission of the souls in purgatory to the will of God* 275

Chapter XV *Reproaches of the soul in purgatory to persons in this world* 276

Chapter XVI *Showing that the sufferings of the souls in purgatory do not prevent their peace and joy.* 277

11

Chapter XVII *Which concludes with an application of all that has been said concerning the souls in purgatory to what the saint experiences in her own soul.* 278

INTRODUCTION

The publication of the Life of St Catherine of Genoa at this moment is, for several reasons, opportune.

The reading of it will correct the misconceptions of many who honestly fancy that the Catholic Church encourages a mechanical piety, fixes the attention of the soul almost, if not altogether, on outward observances, and inculcates nothing beyond a complete submission to her authority and discipline.

The life of our Saint is an example of the reverse of that picture. It makes clear the truth that the immediate guide of the Christian soul is the Holy Spirit, and that her uncommon fidelity to the inspirations of the Holy Spirit, made this holy woman worthy of being numbered by the Church among that class of her most cherished children, who have attained the highest degree of Divine love which it is possible for human beings to reach upon earth.

The mistake of the persons above spoken of arises from their failing to see that the indwelling Holy Spirit is the divine life of the Church, and that her sacraments have for their end to convey the Holy Spirit to the soul. It arises also from their not sufficiently appreciating the necessity of the authority and discipline of the Church, as safeguards to the soul from being led astray from the paths of the Holy Spirit.

Without doubt God could have, if He had so pleased, saved and sanctified the souls of men in spite of their ignorance, perversity, and weakness, by the immediate communication and action of the Holy Spirit in their souls, independently of an external organization like the Church. But such was not His pleasure, or His plan. For His own wise reasons, He chose to establish a Church which He authorized to teach the world whatsoever He had commanded, which He promised to be with unto the end of all time, whose ministry, sacraments, and government should serve Him, as His body had, to continue and complete, by a visible means, the work of man's redemption.

Hence it is an entirely false view of the nature and design of the Church to suppose that it was intended to be, or is in its action, or ever was, or ever can be, a substitute for the authority of Christ, or the immediate guidance of the Holy Spirit in the Christian soul.

The authority of the Church is no other that the authority of Christ, as He Himself has declared, "He that heareth you, heareth Me."[1] The sacraments are nothing else than the channels, or visible means, of communicating the Holy Spirit to the soul. It is the divine action in the Church which gives to its external organization the principal reason for its existence.

And it is equally false, and at the same time absurd, to suppose for a moment that the Holy Spirit indwelling in the Church and embodied in her visible authority, and the same Holy Spirit dwelling in and inspiring the Christian souls, should ever contradict each other, or come into collision. Whenever, by supposition, this takes place, be assured it is not the work of the Holy Spirit, but the consequence of ignorance, error, or perversity on the part of the individual; for it must not be forgotten, or ever be lost sight of, that it pleased Christ our Lord to promise to His Church that "the gates of hell shall not prevail against her,"[2] and not to teach individual Christians.

The test, therefore, of the sincerity of the Christian soul in following the inspirations of the Holy Spirit, will be shown, in case of uncertainty, by its prompt obedience to the voice of the Holy Church. It is only when the soul goes astray from the paths

---

[1] S. Luke x, 16
[2] S . Matthew xvi, 18

2

of the Holy Spirit, it finds trammels to its feet, otherwise it is conscious of perfect liberty in the Church of God.

From the foregoing truths, the following practical rule of safe-conduct can be drawn. The immediate guide of the soul to salvation and sanctification is the Holy Spirit, and the criterion or test that the soul is guided by the Holy Spirit, is its ready obedience to the authority of the Church. With this rule there can be no danger of going astray, and the soul can walk in absolute security, in the ways of sanctity.

This is the way in which all the saints have trod to arrive at Christian perfection, but no life illustrates this truth more plainly, so far as we are aware, than the life of our saint.

There are others who think that the Church fosters a sanctity which is not concerned with this present life, rendering one useless to society, and indifferent to the great needs of humanity.

The love of God and the love of one's neighbor as taught by Christ and His Apostles, are essentially one. If the saints of the Church were distinguished for their great love for God, they ought therefore to be equally distinguished for their great love for mankind. The one is the test of the other. If any man say, "I love God, and hateth his neighbor, he is a liar." Such is the emphatic language of St John.[3]

Let us apply this test, with the history of the Church and the biographies of her saints, in our hands. Take, for example, the religious orders, and it is a fair one, for nearly all of them were founded by saints, whose special aim it was to teach and practice Christian perfection, as understood by the Catholic Church. What do these pages of history and biography teach us? All that we possess of the classics, and of literature in every department, pagan as well as Christian, prior to the invention of the art of printing, we owe exclusively to the industry and labor of the early monks. Not a slight service. These men were for the most

---

[3] 1 Ep. S. John

part the founders and professors of the great universities and colleges in England, Italy, Spain, France, Germany, and Ireland. The last were not the least, for the monks of Ireland were famous as founders of colleges and seats of learning in their own as well as in foreign countries. Monks were the pioneers in agriculture, and in many industrial and mechanical arts, while their monasteries became the centers of great cities, many of which still retain their names. They were the sowers of those seeds, which, being developed by time, men of our day claim all the honor of their results, but modestly, under the title of "modern civilization!"

"Idle monks and nuns" were they? They were, as a class, men and women who ate less, worked harder, and did more for intellectual progress, civilization, and social well-being, than any other body of men and women, whose record can be found on the pages of history, or who can be pointed out in this nineteenth century!

As for works of mercy, such is the superabundance of material, that it is difficult to know where to begin, and how to leave off.

The brotherhoods and sisterhoods in the Church, devoted to the care and relief of the sick, the orphan, the aged, the poor, the captive, the prisoner, the insane, and to the thousand and one ills that human nature is heir to, as well as those which are self-inflicted, who can count them?

True, there were some religious orders which were given almost exclusively to contemplation, but these were exceptional vocations, and were so considered by the Church. These had also a most important social bearing and practical value, which, however, this is not the place to demonstrate. But the great majority of her saints were men and women whose hearts were overflowing with warm and active sympathy for their race, consecrating their energies to its improvement spiritually, intellectually, morally, and bodily, and not seldom laying down their lives for its sake.

That the Church did not compel all her children, seeking Christian perfection, into one uniform type, is true. Governed by that divine wisdom which made man differ from man in his talents and aptitudes, she did not attempt to mar and wrong their nature, but sought to elevate and sanctify each in his own peculiar individuality.

Read the life of Saint Catherine, and in imagination fancy her in the city hospital of Genoa, charged, not only with the supervision and responsibility of its finances, but also overseeing the care of its sick inmates, taking an active, personal part in its duties, as one of its nurses, and the whole establishment conducted with strict economy, perfect order, and the tenderest care and love! Fancy this for a moment in the city hospital of Genoa in the sixteenth century, and seek for her compeer in the city of New York, or in any other city in the world, in our day, and if you find one, and outside of the Catholic Church, then, but not till then, you may repeat to your heart's content, that she fosters a sanctity which turns one's attention altogether away from this world, and makes one indifferent to the wants of humanity.

Saint Catherine's life teaches another lesson to those whose mental eyes are not closed to facts as plain as the sun when shining at noonday.

We hear much said, and not a little is written, in the United States and in England, about the exclusion of woman from spheres of action for which her natural aptitudes fit her equally, and in many cases render her superior to men; of her partial education, and in many cases, the inferior position which she is forced to accept in society.

Strange that we hear no such complaints in Catholic society, or from Catholic women! Is it because they have been taught to hug the chains which make them slaves? or that they are denied the liberty of speech? or that their lips are closed by arbitrary authority? Not at all. The reason is plain. Women, no less than men, are free to occupy any position whose duties and functions

5

they have the intelligence or aptitude to fulfill. They have the opportunities and are free to obtain the highest education their capacities are capable of. This, every Catholic woman knows and feels, and hence the absence of all consciousness, in the Church, of being deprived of her rights, of oppression, and injustice.

One has but to open his eyes and read the pages of ecclesiastical history to be convinced that in the Catholic Church there has been no lack of freedom of action for women. Look for a moment at the countless number of sisterhoods in the Church, some counting their members by thousands, all under the government of one head, a woman, and elected by themselves for life. Others again, each house forming a separate organization, with a superior of its own, elected for a limited period. In fact, there is no form of organization and government, of which they do not give us an example, and carried on successfully, showing a practical ability in this field of action, which no one can call in question. Then, there is no kind of labor, literary, scientific, mechanical, as well as charitable, in which they may not engage, according to their abilities and strength. Who shall enumerate the different kinds of literary institutions, schools, and academies under their direction, and confessedly superior in their kind? Who shall count the hospitals, the orphanages, the reformatories, the insane asylums, and other similar institutions, where they have proved their capacity to be above that of men? All roads are open to woman's energies and capacities in the Church, and she knows and is conscious of this freedom; and what is more, she is equally aware that whatever she has ability to do, will receive from the Church encouragement, sanction, and that honor which is due to her labor, her devotion, and her genius.

Few great undertakings in the Church have been conceived and carried on to success, without the cooperation, in some shape, of women. The great majority of her saints are of their sex, and they are honored and placed on her altars equally with men. It is not an unheard of event, that women, by their

6

scientific and literary attainments, have won from Catholic Universities the title of Doctor. Saint Teresa is represented as an authorized teacher, with a pen in hand, and with a doctor's cap. It would carry us altogether too far beyond the limits of this preface to show how largely the writings of women in the Church, have contributed to the body and perfection of the science of theology.

In this respect also, our saint was distinguished. Her spiritual dialogues and her treatise on purgatory have been recognized by those competent to judge in such matters, as masterpieces in spiritual literature. Saint Francis of Sales, that great master in spiritual life, in whose city we have the consolation of writing this preface, was accustomed to read the latter twice a year. Frederic Schlegel, who was the first to translate Saint Catherine's dialogues into German, regarded them as seldom if ever equaled in beauty of style; and such has been the effect of the example of Christian perfection in our saint, that even the "American Tract Society" could not resist its attraction, and published a short sketch of her life among its tracts, with the title of her name by marriage, Catherine Adorno.

It was fitting that the life of Saint Catherine of Genoa should be translated for the first time into English, by one who is now no more, but who was while living, distinguished, like our saint, for her intellectual gifts, for her charity toward the poor and abandoned, and in consecrating her pen to the cause and glory of God's Church.

L. T. HECKER

Annecy, Oct. 7, 1873

7

LIFE AND DOCTRINE OF SAINT CATHERINE OF GENOA

CHAPTER I

Of the parents and ancestors of the blessed Catherine, and how at eight years of age she began to do penance; her gift of prayer, and of her desire to enter into religion, and her marriage against her will.

Catherine was born at Genoa in the year 1447. Her parents, Giacopo Fieschi and Francesca di Negro, daughter of Sigismund, Marquis di Negro, were both of illustrious and noble birth. On account of his merits, her father (a descendant of Robert, brother of Pope Innocent IV, who was uncle of another Pontiff, Adrian V) was created Viceroy of Naples, under King Regnier, in which office he remained until his death.

Although of very noble parentage, and very delicate and beautiful in person, yet from her earliest years, she despised the pride of birth, and abhorred luxury; so that when only about eight years of age, she was inspired with the desire to do penance, and beginning to dislike the soft indulgence of her bed, she laid herself down humbly to sleep on straw, with a block of hard wood under her head, in the place of pillows of down.

She had in her chamber that image of our Lord, which is commonly called "La Pieta," and whenever she entered there, and raised her eyes to it, a violent pain seized her whole frame, caused by her grief and love at the thought of what our Lord had suffered for love of us.

She led a very simple life, seldom speaking with any one, very obedient to her parents, well skilled in the way of the divine precepts, and zealous in the practice of the virtues.

At the age of twelve, God in his grace bestowed on her the gift of prayer, and a wonderful communion with our Lord, which enkindled within her a new flame of deep love, together with a lively sense of the sufferings he endured in his holy passion, with many other good inclinations for the things of God.

At the age of thirteen, she was inspired with a desire for the religious life, and immediately communicated this inspiration to her spiritual father, who was also confessor to the devout convent of our Lady of Grace, in which she desired to become a nun, together with her pious sister Limbania. She earnestly begged the Father to make known her holy desire to the superiors of the convent above mentioned, and urge that they would deign to receive her into their company. When this prudent, spiritual father saw and heard such love for religion in one of so tender and delicate age, he began to represent to her the austerities of the religious life; the innumerable temptations of the enemy; the delicacy of her body, and many other things, to all of which Catherine answered with so much prudence and zeal, that the father was astonished, for her replies did not appear to him human, but supernatural and divine; and he therefore promised her that he would lay the matter before the superiors, which he did on the following day, at the same time communicating to them the prudent, remarkable answers of his spiritual daughter to his disclosures concerning the temptations and austerities of the religious life. After taking his proposal into deliberate consideration the superiors of the convent replied, that they were not accustomed to receive among them girls of so tender an age. To this the Father made answer that judgment and devotion not only supplied the want of age, but were better than years; still, they judged it inexpedient to receive her as it was contrary to their custom, which decision greatly afflicted the young girl who still trusted that Almighty God would not abandon her.

At the age of sixteen, she was married by her parents to a young Genoese of noble family, named, Giuliano Adorno; and although this step was contrary to her wishes, yet her great simplicity, submission, and reverence for her parents gave her patience to endure it.

But God, who in his goodness would not leave his chosen one to place her affections on the world and the flesh, permitted a husband to be given her entirely the opposite of herself in his mode of life, who caused her so much suffering, that for ten years, she could hardly support life, and by his imprudence she was at length reduced to poverty.

The last five of these ten years she devoted to external affairs, and feminine amusements, seeking solace for her hard life, as women are prone to do, in the diversions and vanities of the world, yet not to a sinful extent; and she did this, because, during the five first years, she suffered inconsolably from sadness; this was constantly increased by the opposition of her husband's disposition to her own, which distressed her so much, that one day, (it was the vigil of St Benedict), having gone into the church of that saint, in her grief she exclaimed: "Pray to God for me, Oh, St Benedict, that for three months he may keep me sick in bed." This she said almost in desperation, not knowing what to do, so great was her distress of mind; for during the three months before her conversion she was overwhelmed with mental suffering, and filled with deep disgust for all things belonging to the world; wherefore, she shunned the society of every one. She was oppressed with a melancholy quite insupportable to herself, and took no interest in anything.

But after these ten years she was called by God and converted in a marvelous manner, as will appear hereafter.

CHAPTER II

She is wounded with divine love in the presence of her confessor. Manifestations of the love of God and of her own offences. The Lord appears to her carrying his cross, and she is taken up three degrees toward God.

The day following the feast of St Benedict, Catherine, at the instance of her sister, who was a nun, went to confession at the convent of the latter, although she had no desire to do so; but her sister said to her: "At least go to obtain the blessing of our confessor," for he was indeed a holy man. The moment she knelt before him, she was wounded so forcibly with the love of God, and received so clear a revelation of her misery and faults, and of the goodness of God, that she had well nigh fallen to the ground.

Overpowered by these emotions, and by her sense of the offences she had committed against her dear Lord, she was so drawn away by her purified affections from the miseries of the world, that she became almost beside herself; and without ceasing, internally repented to herself, in the ardor of love: "No more would, no more sin." And at that moment if she had possessed a thousand worlds, she would have thrown them all away.

Through the ardent flame of burning love with which she was enkindled, her good God, by his grace, impressed instantly upon that soul, and infused into it, all perfection, purging it of all earthly affections, illuminating it with a divine light by which she was enabled to perceive with her interior eye, his goodness; and in a word, united her with himself, and changed and transformed her entirely by the true union of a good will, inflaming her wholly with his burning love.

The saint while in the presence of her confessor lost entirely all consciousness through this sweet wound of love, so that she could not speak; but her confessor was not yet aware of this when he chanced to be called out, and left her so overwhelmed with grief and love, that she said to him, with great difficulty, when he returned: "With your consent, father, I will leave my confession till another time;" and she did so. Returning home, she was so on fire and wounded with the love which God had interiorly manifested to her, together with the view of her miseries, that, as if beside herself, she went into a private chamber, and gave vent to her burning tears and sighs.

At that moment she was instructed interiorly in prayer, but her lips could only utter: "oh Love! can it be that you have called me with so much love, and revealed to me at one view, what no tongue can describe?" For many days she could only utter herself in sighs, and wonderfully deep they were; and so great was her contrition for her offences against such infinite goodness, that if she had not been miraculously supported, her heart would have broken, and she would have died.

But when our Lord saw this soul still more interiorly inflamed with his love, and filled with sorrow for her sins, he appeared to her in spirit, with the cross upon his shoulder, dripping with blood which she saw was shed wholly for love, and this vision so inflamed her heart, that she was more than ever lost in love and grief.

This vision made such an impression upon her that she seemed always to see with her bodily eyes, her bleeding Love, nailed to the cross. Very plainly too did she see all the offences she had committed against him, and cried out continually: "Oh Love, no more sin, no more sin!" Her hatred of herself became so great, that filled with disgust she exclaimed: "Oh Love, if it be necessary I am prepared to make a public confession of my sins."

After this she made her general confession with such contrition and compunction, that her soul was at once cleansed of its sins, for God had pardoned them all, consuming them in the flames of love, with which he had already wounded her heart; yet, to satisfy justice he led her through the way of satisfaction, permitting that this contrition and self-knowledge should continue for nearly fourteen months; and when she had made satisfaction, relieved her of the sight of her sins so entirely that she never beheld again the least of them, no more than if they had all been cast into the depths of the sea.

At that moment of her vocation, when she was wounded at the feet of her confessor, she seemed to be drawn to the feet of our Lord Jesus Christ, and in spirit beheld all the graces, means, and ways, by which the Lord, in his pure love, had brought her to conversion. In this light she remained for more than a year, relieving her conscience by means of contrition, confession, and satisfaction.

She felt herself drawn with St. John, to rest on the bosom of her loving Lord, and there she discovered a sweeter way which contained in itself many secrets of the bounteous love which was consuming her, so that she was often beside herself; and in her intense eagerness, her hatred of self, and her deep contrition, she would lick the earth with her tongue, and so great was the wain of contrition, and the sweetness of love, that she knew not what she was doing; but she felt her heart lightened, occupied with unbounded, poignant grief, and the sweet ardor of love. Thus she remained for three years or more, melted with love and grief, and with the deep and burning flames that were consuming her heart.

Then she was drawn to the open wound in the side of the crucified Lord, and there she was allowed to see the Sacred heart of her Lord burning with the same flames with which her own was enkindled; at the sight of this, her heart died within her, and her strength abandoned her. This impression remained for many years which were spent by her, in continual sighs, and burning flames, so that her heart and soul were well nigh melted, and she was constrained to cry out: "I have no longer either soul or heart;

14

but my soul and my heart are those of my Beloved;" and in him she was wholly absorbed and transformed.

Finally, her sweet and loving Lord drew her to himself, and bestowed upon her a caress, by the power of which she was entirely immersed in that sweet Divinity to which she abandoned herself exteriorly, so that she exclaimed: "I live no longer, but Christ lives in me." She knew no longer whether her mere human acts were good or bad, but saw all things in God.

CHAPTER III

How the desire was given her to receive holy communion, and of its precious effects in her; of her sufferings when she did not receive, and how it seemed to her that she had lost faith, and walked by sight.

On the day of the Festival of the Annunciation of the glorious Virgin Mary, after her conversion, that is, after her loving wound, her Lord gave her the desire for holy communion, which she never lost during her whole life; and her Love ordered it in such a way, that communion was given her, without any care on her part, for she was, in a wonderful manner, provided with it in one way or another; and without asking, she was often summoned to receive it, by priests inspired by God to give it to her.

On one occasion a holy religious said to her: "You receive communion every day, how are you now satisfied?" and she answered him simply, explaining her desires and feelings. In order to prove her, he said to her: "Perhaps there may be something wrong in receiving communion so often" and then left her. In consequence of this, Catherine, for fear of doing wrong, abstained from communion, but with great pain; and the religious, finding that she thought more of doing wrong, than of the consolation and satisfaction of communion, directed her to make daily communion, and she returned to her accustomed way.

Once, when at the point of death, so ill that she was unable to take any sustenance, she said to her confessor: "If you would give me my Lord three times only, I should be cured." It was done, and her health was immediately restored. Before receiving communion, she suffered severe pains about the heart, and said:

"My heart is not like that of others, for it only rejoices in its Lord; and therefore give him to me." It indeed seemed that otherwise she could not have lived, and if deprived of communion, her life would have consumed away in suffering. Of this there are many proofs, for if, on any day, she happened not to receive, she would pass it in almost insupportable pain, so that her attendants were filled with compassion for her, and believed it clearly, to be the will of God, that she should receive daily.

One day, after communion, God gave her such consolation, that she lost her consciousness, and the priest could not give her the ablution until she had been restored to herself, and she then exclaimed: "Oh, Lord, I do not desire to follow thee for these consolations, but only for pure love."

Although she did not easily shed tears she awoke one night weeping, when she had dreamed that she was not to receive on the next day. But if, for any human reason, she could not have received it, she would have been patient and confident, saying to her Lord: "If thou wouldst, it could be given to me."

She said, that at the beginning of her conversion, when this desire of communion was first given to her, she sometimes envied the priests who received whenever they wished, without causing remarks from any one. And it was her special desire, to be able to say the three masses on Christmas day; so that she envied no one in this world but the priests, and when she saw the Sacrament in the hands of one of them at the altar, she would say within herself: "Take it, take it quickly, to your heart, for it is the Lord of the heart." To receive it, she would have gone miles, and endured fatigues beyond human power to bear.

When she was at mass she was often so occupied interiorly with her Lord, that she did not hear a word; but when the time came to receive communion she accused herself, and would say: "Oh! my Lord, it seems to me that if I were dead, I should come to life, in order to receive thee, and if an unconsecrated host were given to me, that I should know it by the taste, as one

17

knows wine from water." She said this, because, when consecrated, it sent a certain ray of love into the very depths of her heart.

She also said, that if she had seen the whole court of heaven, arrayed in such a manner, that there was no difference between God and the angels, yet the love in her heart would have caused her to know God, as the dog knows his master: and much sooner, and with less effort, because love, which is God, himself, instantly and directly finds its end, and last repose.

At one time, on receiving, she perceived such an odor and such sweetness, that she believed herself in Paradise, when suddenly she turned towards her Lord, and humbly said: "O Lord perhaps thou wouldst draw me to thee by this fragrance? I do not desire it; I desire nothing but thee, and thee wholly; thou knowest, that from the beginning I have asked of thee the grace that I might never see visions, nor receive external consolations, for so clearly do I perceive thy goodness, that I do not seem to walk by faith but by a true and heartfelt experience."

CHAPTER IV

How she was unable to take food during Lent and Advent, being sustained by the Blessed Sacrament

Some time after her conversion, on the day the Annunciation of our Lady, her Love spoke within her, saying, that he wished her to keep the fast in his company in the desert, and immediately she became unable to eat, so that she was without food for the body until Easter, and with the exception of the three fast days, on which she had the grace to be able to eat, she took nothing during the whole of Lent.

She afterwards ate, as at other times, without disgust; and in this manner she passed twenty-three Lents and as many Advents, during which time she took nothing but a tumblerful of water, vinegar, and pounded salt. When she drank this mixture, it seemed as if it were thrown upon a red-hot surface, and that it was at once dried up in the great fire that was burning within her. How wonderful! for no one, however healthy, could bear a drink of this kind, fasting; but she described the sweetness that proceeded from her burning heart, as so great, that even this harsh beverage refreshed her.

This rejection of food, at first, gave her great trouble, for now knowing the cause, she suspected some deception; but when she, again and again, forced herself to take food, and her stomach rejected it, all her family, as well as herself, regarded it as a prodigy; for even when she attempted to eat, in obedience to her confessor, the result was the same.

This was the more remarkable, because at other times she could eat and retain her food, even up to the very day when Lent and Advent began. During the seasons when she could not eat, she practiced pious works more than at other times, she slept better, and felt stronger and more active; and she also went to table with the others, to avoid, as far as possible, all singularity; and even forced herself to taste something, in order to escape observation; then she would say to herself: "Oh if you knew what I feel within!" By this she meant the burning and pure love, and union with God, which those around her could hardly endure, so much were they astonished that she could not eat; but she paid no heed to them, saying to herself: "If we regarded the operations of God, we should look at the interior more than the exterior. Living without food is purely an operation of God, without my will; but it is nothing to boast of, or to cause surprise, for to him it is as nothing. The pure light shows us, that we should not regard the manifestations that God makes of himself for our necessities and his own glory, but only the pure love with which his divine majesty performs his work in our behalf, and the soul becoming these pure operations of a love which looks for no good that we can do, must needs love him purely, without regard to any particular grace which she receives from him, but looking to him alone, for himself alone, who is worthy of being loved without measure, and with no reference either to soul or body."

CHAPTER V

Of her great penances and mortifications

During the first four years after she had received the sweet wound from her Lord, she performed many penances, and mortified all her senses. She deprived her nature of all that it desired, and obliged it to take what it disliked. She wore hair-cloth, and ate no meat, nor fruit of any kind, either fresh or dry; and being by nature courteous and affable, she did great violence to herself, by conversing as little as possible with her relatives when they visited her, without any respect to herself or to them; and if any one was surprised by it, she took no notice.

She practiced great austerity in sleeping, lying down on sharply pointed things. As soon as she determined to do any thing, she never felt any temptation to the contrary. The fire within was so great, that she took no account of exterior things relating to the body, although she neglected no necessary work; and no temptations except those of her natural inclinations could affect her. This was the case throughout her whole after-life. She so resisted her natural inclinations, that they were completely destroyed. Temptations like insects, could not approach the flames of pure love enkindled in her heart.

Her eyes were always cast down. During the first four years of her conversion she spent six hours daily in prayer, for such was the obedience of her body to the spirit, that it dared not rebel, although it suffered keenly; and she thus fulfilled in herself the words: cor meum, et caro meo, exultaverunt in Deum vivum.

During these first four years, the interior fire that was consuming her produced such extreme hunger, and so quickly did she digest her food, that she could have devoured iron. She comprehended that this desire for food was something supernatural. She was also unable to speak except in so low a tone as scarcely to be understood, so powerful was her interior feeling.

Most of the time she appeared like one beside herself, for she neither spoke, nor heard, nor tasted nor valued any thing in the world; neither did she look at any thing.

Yet she lived in subjection to every one, and was always more inclined to do the will of others than her own. And it is remarkable, that although God even in the beginning made her perfect by infused grace, so that she was at once entirely purified in her affections, illuminated and peaceful in her intellect, and transformed in all things by his sweet love, yet it was the will of God, that the divine justice should be observed in the mortification of all her senses, which, although they were already mortified, so far as regarded the consent to any natural inclinations, even the slightest, yet the Lord allowed her to see what these were, and therefore, she very carefully opposed them.

She was sometimes asked, when practicing such mortifications of all her senses: "Why are you doing this?" And she answered: "I do not know, but I feel myself interiorly and irresistibly drawn to do so, and I believe that this is the will of God; but it is not his will that I should have any object in it." And it seemed indeed to be the truth, for, at the end of four years, all these mortifications ended, so that if she still wished to practice them, she could no longer have done so.

At that time, listening one day to a sermon in which the conversion of Mary Magdalen was narrated, she heard a voice in her heart saying: "I understand;" and by her correspondence with the preaching, she perceived her conversion to have been like that of Magdalen.

CHAPTER VI

How she was withdrawn by God from the use of her senses. Of three rules given her by the Lord, and of certain words chosen from the Our Father and Hail Mary, and from the whole of the Holy Scripture.

After the four years above mentioned, her mind became clear and free, and so filled with God that nothing else ever entered into it. At mass and instructions her bodily senses were closed; but interiorly, in the divine light, she saw and heard many things, being wholly absorbed in secret delights; and it was not in her power to do otherwise.

It is wonderful, that with all this interior occupation, God did not allow her to depart from the usual order. Whenever it was needful, she returned to her accustomed mode of life, answered the questions put to her, and thus she gave no cause of complaint to any one.

She was sometimes so lost in the sense of divine love, that she was obliged to hide herself, for she was like one dead. In order to escape such a condition, she endeavored to remain in the company of others, and said to her Lord: "I wish not, O sweet Love, for that which proceeds from thee, but for thyself alone!" She wished to love God without soul and without body, and unsustained by them, with a direct, pure, and sincere, love; but the more she shunned these consolations, the more her Lord bestowed them upon her. Sometimes she was found in a remote place, prostrate on the earth, her face covered with her hands, so completely lost in the sweetness of divine love, that she was insensible to the loudest cry.

At other times she would walk back and forth, as if lost to self, and following the attraction of love.

Sometimes, when she had been thus lifeless for the space of six hours, she would be aroused suddenly by the voices of persons calling her, and attend to their smallest wants, for she abandoned as hateful all right to self. On these occasions she came forth from her retirement, with a glowing countenance, like a cherub ready to exclaim: "Who will separate me from the love of God," with all the other words of that glorious apostle.

Her love once said to her interiorly: "My daughter, observe these three rules, namely: never say I will or I will not. Never say mine, but always ours. Never excuse yourself, but always accuse yourself." Moreover he said to her: "When you repeat the 'Our Father' take always for your maxim, Fiat voluntas tua, that is, may his will be done in everything that may happen to you, whether good or ill; from the 'Hail Mary' take the word Jesus, and may it be implanted in your heart, and it will be a sweet guide and shield to you in all the necessities of life. And from the rest of Scripture take always for your support this word, Love, with which you will go on your way, direct, pure, light, watchful, quick, enlightened, without erring, yet without a guide or help from any creature; for love needs no support, being sufficient to do all things without fear; neither does love ever become weary, for even martyrdom is sweet to it. And, finally, this love will consume all the inclinations of the soul, and the desires of the body, for the things of this life."

CHAPTER VII

How even her humanity was affected by the burning fire of this love; how much she desired to die, and took delight in hearing masses, bells, and offices, for the dead.

When the use of her senses and facilities was thus lost, in her spiritual joy she said to her humanity: "Are you satisfied with being thus fed?" And humanity answered: "Yes," and that she would sacrifice every enjoyment in this life for it. What must have been the joys of the soul, if even humanity, so contrary to the spirit, also took delight in peace and union with God?

This was the case from the beginning, but at last, that burning, interior flame burst forth, and caused a corresponding suffering in the body, so that she was often obliged to press her hand upon her heart for relief. She could not have endured these pains for two successive days, and after their intensity had passed away, her heart was left melted in a divine and wonderful sweetness.

God allowed her to remain for some days, in this state, and then permitted her to be assailed by another and still more violent attach, so that humanity, rather than take food, would have suffered martyrdom; therefore, when she looked on the dead, or heard offices and masses, or even a passing bell, she rejoiced as if she were going to behold that truth which she experienced in her heart; and she would rather have died than live separated from those things in which she found her support and consolation.

She became reduced to such a condition, that she had no rest but when she slept; and then she felt herself freed from prison, because her attention was not so continually riveted on God. Her desire for death remained for nearly two years, and she was always asking for it, saying: "O cruel death, why do you keep me so anxiously waiting for you?" This desire knew no why, nor how, and it continued until she began to make daily communion.

Filled with this desire, she addressed death, as "Gentle death, sweet, gracious, beautiful, strong, rich, precious, death," and by every other name of honor and dignity that she could call to mind, and then added: "I find, O death, but one fault in thee, thou art too sparing of thyself to him who desires thee, and too ready for him who shuns thee; yet I see that thou dost all things, according to the will of God, which is without fault; but our irregular appetites do not correspond, for if they did so, they would rest on the divine will, in peace and silence, as death itself does, and we should have no more choice than if we were already dead and buried." But she said, it really seemed, if there were any choice for her, that death was the thing to be chosen, because thus the soul is secure from ever offering any hindrance to pure love, and is liberated from the prison of this wretched body and of the world, which, with all their power, are continually engaging her, in every way, in their own occupations, while she regards them as her enemies to which she is outwardly subjected.

When she was performing cruel penances, the sensitive nature never opposed her, but was entirely obedient; but when inflamed with love, it was wonderful how restive it became, and how much it suffered. And for this reason, because in penances the spirit corresponded to humanity, and strengthened her for her share in the work, but afterwards, the spirit being separated from visible things, and God operating in it without means, humanity was left in abandonment, and suffered intolerably without any help. Humanity is indeed capable of penance, but is not capable of such burning love.

But everything was regulated by her merciful God, with the highest wisdom, which enabled the body to endure the most severe penance, and to live and rejoice in these agonizing flames, without complaining; and no one can know how severe is this suffering, unless he has himself experienced it.

CHAPTER VIII

How the Saint devoted herself to pious works, and served in a hospital.

In the beginning of her conversion she devoted herself to good works, seeking for the poor throughout the city, under the guidance of the Ladies of Mercy on whom devolved this charge and who, according to the custom of the city, supplied her with money and provisions for the poor. She cleansed their houses from the most disgusting filth, and she would even put it in her mouth, in order to conquer the disgust it produced. She took home the garments of the poor, covered with dirt and vermin, and having cleansed them thoroughly, returned them to their owners. It was remarkable that nothing unclean was ever found upon herself: she also tended the sick with most devoted affection, speaking to them of their spiritual as well as of their temporal affairs.

She took charge of the great hospital of Genoa, where nothing escaped her watchful care, although her incessant occupations never diminished her affection for God, her sweet Love; neither did this love ever cause her to neglect her service in the hospital, which was regarded as a miracle by all who saw her. It is also remarkable that she never made the mistake of a single farthing, in the accounts of large sums of money which she was obliged to keep, and, for her own little necessities, she made use of her own little income.

There was once in the hospital a very pious woman of the third order of St. Francis, who was dying of a malignant fever. She was in her agony for eight days, and during that time, Catherine often visited her, and would say to her: "Call Jesus!" Unable to articulate, she moved her lips so that it was conjectured that she tried to do so, and Catherine, when she saw her mouth so filled, as it were, with Jesus, could not restrain herself from kissing her, and in this way took the fever, and only narrowly escaped death. This, however, did not diminish her zeal in the service of the hospital, to which she returned immediately upon her recovery, and devoted herself to it with great care and diligence.

CHAPTER IX

Of her wonderful knowledge of God and of herself.

This servant of God had an almost incredible knowledge of herself. She was so purified and enlightened, so united with and transformed into God, her Love, that what she said seemed to be uttered not by a human tongue, but rather by one angelic and divine; which proves the truth that humble souls, thirsting after God, can often grasp what the mere human intellect can never attain or comprehend. She was accustomed to say: "If it were possible for me to suffer as much as all the martyrs have suffered, and even hell itself, for the love of God, and in order to make satisfaction to him, it would be after all only a sort of injury to God, in comparison with the love and goodness with which he has created, and redeemed, and, in a special manner, called me. For man, unassisted by God's grace, is even worse than the devil, because the devil is a spirit without a body, while man, without the grace of God, is a devil incarnate. Man has a free will, which, according to the ordination of God, is in nowise bound, so that he can do all the evil that he wills; to the devil, this is impossible, since he can act only by the divine permission; and when man surrenders to him his evil will, the devil employs it, as the instrument of his temptation."

And hence she said: "I see that whatever is good in myself, in any other creature, or in the saints, is truly from God; if, on the other hand, I do any thing evil, it is I alone who do it, nor can I charge the blame of it upon the devil or upon any other creature; it is purely the work of my own will, inclination, pride, selfishness, sensuality, and other evil dispositions, without the help of God I should never do any good thing. So sure am I of this, that if all the angels of heaven were to tell me I have something good in me, I should not believe them."

This holy soul knew in what true perfection consists, and had, moreover a knowledge of all imperfections. There is nothing surprising in this, for her interior eye was enlightened, her affections purified, and her heart wholly united to God, her Love, in whom she saw things wonderful and hidden from human sense. She said, therefore: "So long as any one can speak of divine things, enjoy and understand them, remember and desire them, he has not yet arrived in port; yet there are ways and means to guide him thither. But the creature can know nothing but what God gives him to know from day to day, nor can he comprehend beyond this, and at each instant remains satisfied with what he receives. If the creature knew the height to which God is prepared to raise him in this life, he would never rest, but on the contrary would feel a certain craving, a vehement desire to reach quickly that ultimate perfection, and would think himself in hell until he had obtained it."

Even at the beginning of her conversion, this holy and devout soul, inflamed with divine love, was wont to exclaim: "Oh! Lord, I desire thee wholly, for in thy clear and strong light I see that the soul can never be at peace until she has attained her last perfection. Oh, sweet Lord! if I believed that I should lose one spark of thee, I could no longer live." Again she said: "It appeared to me, as I noted from time to time, that the love wherewith I loved my sweet Love, grew greater day by day, and yet, at each step, I had thought it as perfect as it could be, for love has this property that it can never perceive in itself the least defect. But as my vision grew clearer, I beheld in myself many imperfections which, had I seen them in the beginning, I should have esteemed nothing, not even hell itself, too great or painful that would have rid me of them. In the beginning they were hidden from me, for it was the purpose of God to accomplish his work by little and little, in order to keep me humble, and enable me to remain among my fellow creatures. And finally, seeing a completed work entirely beyond the creature, I am compelled to say what before I could not say, and confess how clear it is to me that all our works are even more imperfect than any creature can fully understand."

This holy creature was accustomed to use the words: "Sweetness of God; purity of God," and other beautiful expressions of the same kind. Sometimes she uttered expressions like these: "I see without eyes, hear without understanding, feel without feeling, and taste without tasting. I know neither form nor measure; for without seeing I yet behold an operation so divine that the words I first used, perfection, purity, and the like seem to me now mere lies in the presence of the truth. The sun which once looked so bright is now dark; what was sweet is now bitter, because sweetness and beauty are spoiled by contact with creatures. Nor can I any longer say: 'My God, my All.' Everything is mine, for all that is God's seems to be wholly mine. Neither in heaven nor on earth shall I ever again use such words, for I am mute and lost in God. Nor can I call the saints blessed, nor the blessed holy, for I see that their sanctity and their beatitude is not theirs, but exists only in God. I see nothing good or blessed in any creature if it be not wholly annihilated and absorbed in God, so that he alone may remain in the creature and the creature in him.

"This is the beatitude that the blessed might have, and yet they have it not, except in so far as they are dead to themselves and absorbed in God. They have it not in so far as they remain in themselves and can say: 'I am blessed.' Words are wholly inadequate to express my meaning, and I reproach myself for using them. I would that every one could understand me, and I am sure that if I could breathe on creatures, the fire of love burning within me would inflame them all with divine desire. O thing most marvelous! So great is my love for God, that beside it all love for the neighbor seems only hypocrisy. I can no longer condescend to creatures, or if I do so, it is only with pain, for to me the world seems only to live in vanity."

CHAPTER X

How impossible it was for vain-glory to enter the mind of this holy creature. Of the light which hatred of self gave her, and of the value of our own actions.

Vain-glory could never enter her mind, for she had seen the truth, and distrusting herself, placed her whole confidence in God, saying always: "Oh Lord! do with me what thou wilt." She had so little esteem of herself that it was pleasing to her to be reproved for any inclination she might have, nor did she ever excuse herself. So clear was the interior vision of that illuminated mind, and such deep things did she say concerning perfection that she could hardly be understood except by the most profound intellects. Among other things she said: "I would not wish to see one meritorious act attributed to myself, even if it were the means of insuring my salvation; for I should be worse than a demon, to wish to rob God of his own. Yet it is needful that we ourselves act, for the divine grace neither vivifies nor aids that which does not work itself, and grace will not save us without our cooperation. I repeat it; all works, without the help of grace are dead, being produced by the creature only; but grace aids all works performed by those who are not in mortal sin, and makes them worthy of heaven; not those which are ours solely, but those in which grace cooperates." So jealous was she for the glory of God, that she was wont to say: "If I could find any good in any creature, (which, however, is impossible) I would tear it from her, and restore it all to God."

Chapter XI

Of the revelation she had concerning purity of conscience, and of the opposition of sin to God.

Illuminated by a clear ray from the true light which shone into this holy soul she spoke admirable things concerning purity of conscience, saying: "Purity of conscience can endure nothing but God only; for he alone is spotless, simple, pure: of all things else, that is, of what is evil, it cannot endure even the smallest spark; this can neither be understood nor appreciated, if it be not felt." Hence she had ever in her mouth, as a habit, this word Purity: she had also a cleanliness and purity most admirable in her speech. She wished that every conception and emotion of the mind should issue to from it undefiled and pure, without the least complexity, and thus it was impossible for her to feign a sympathy she did not feel, or to condole with others out of friendship, except so far as she really corresponded with them in her heart. The continual humility, contempt, and hatred of self, in this soul were at this time most remarkable. When, by the divine permission, she suffered such mental distress that she could scarcely open her mouth, she would then say: "Oh, Love! let me remain thus, that I may be submissive; for otherwise it would be impossible that I should not do something wrong. Oh, how good and admirable is the knowledge of a soul, which, being all protected, united, and transformed in God, her felicity, sees clearly, on one side, her own inclination to all that is evil, and on the other, how she is restrained by God, that she may not commit actual sin! One thing is certain; namely, that never is the soul so perfect that it does not need the continual help of God, even though it be transformed in him. It is true, that the nature of the sweet God is such, that he never allows these souls to fall, although the soul, left to herself, could fall if she were not thus restrained. But he only preserves those who never with their free will consent unto sin; and allows those to fall who do voluntarily yield assent thereto; for truly, having given us free will, he will not force it. Consequently, those who fall into sin do so by their own fault, and not by that of God, who is ever ready to aid the soul even after her fall, if she will allow herself to be aided, and will correspond to the divine grace which never ceases to call her, saying: 'Turn from evil and do good, and be converted to me with your whole heart.'"

And therefore she said: "If the soul, fallen into what sins soever, corresponds to the grace of God and abhors her past sins, with a resolution and a will to sin no more, he immediately frees her from her guilt, and holds her so that she may not fall, nor through her own malice be separated from him, that is, from the observance of his commandments which are his will; to sin voluntarily, is to be separated from God. And not only is he ready, on his own part to do all this, but I see clearly with the interior eye, that the sweet God loves with a pure love the creature that he has created, and has a hatred for nothing but sin, which is more opposed to him than can be thought or imagined. I say, God loves his creature with a perfection that cannot be understood, nor could it be even by an angelic intellect which would fail to comprehend even its slightest spark. And if God wished to make a soul understand, it would be necessary to give her an immortal body, since by nature it could never endure the knowledge. For it is impossible that God and sin, however slight, should remain together, for such an impediment would prevent the soul from attaining to his glory. And as a little thing that thou hast in thine eye will not allow thee to see the sun, and as it is possible to compare the difference between God and the sun to that between the intellectual vision and that of the bodily eye, it is plain that the great opposition between the one and the other can never be truly imagined.

"Wherefore, it is necessary that the soul which desires to be preserved from sin in this life, and to glorify God in the other,

35

should be spotless, pure, and simple, and not voluntarily retain a single thing which is not purged by contrition, confession and satisfaction, because all our works are imperfect and defective. Whence, if I consider and observe clearly, with the interior eye, I see that I ought to live entirely detached from self; Love has wished me to understand this, and in a manner I do understand it, so that I could not possibly be deceived; and for my part I have so abandoned myself, that I can regard it only as a demon, or worse, if I may so say."

"After God has given a soul the light in which she perceives the truth that she cannot even will, and much less work, apart from him, without always soiling and making turbid the clear waters of his grace, then she sacrifices all to him, and he takes possession of his creature, and both inwardly and outwardly occupies her with himself, so that she can do nothing but as her sweet Love wills. Then the soul, by reason of its union with God, contradicts Him in nothing, nor does aught but what is pure, upright, gentle, sweet, and delightful, because God allows nothing to molest it. And these are the works which please the Lord our God."

CHAPTER XII

Of the great and solicitous care which God operates in divers ways in order to attract the soul to himself, so that he seems to be in a manner our servant.—Of the blindness of man.—Of the many ways in which he is deceived by his own self-will.

"I see that the sweet God is so solicitous for the welfare of the soul, that no human being could have a like anxiety to gain the whole world even if he were certain to obtain it by his efforts; when behold the love he displays in providing us with all possible aids to lead us into heaven, I am, as it were, forced to say that this sweet Master appears as if he were our servant. If man could see the care which God takes of a soul, nothing more would be necessary to amaze and confound him than to consider that this glorious God, in whom all things have their being, should have so great a providence over his creatures; yet we, to whom it is a matter either of salvation or damnation, hold it in light esteem."

"But alas! how can this be so? If we esteem not that which God esteems, what else should we esteem? O wretched man, where dost thou lose thyself? What dost thou with that time, so precious, of which thou hast such need? What with those goods with which thou shouldst buy Paradise? What with thy body, which was given thee to work for and to serve thy soul? What with thy soul, whose end is to be united to God by love? All these thou hast turned towards earth, which produces a seed whose fruits thou wilt eat with the demons in hell with infinite despair, because, having lost that glory for which thou wert created, and to which so many inspirations called thee, thou wilt then see that thou hast failed to secure it through thine own fault alone.

"Know for a certainty that if men understood how terrible is even one solitary sin, they would rather be cast into a heated furnace, and there remain, living both in soul and body, than to support such a sight. And if the sea were all fire they would cast themselves therein and never leave it, if they were certain of meeting the sin on doing so." To many this will appear a strange saying, but to the saint these things had been shown as in truth they were, and such a comparison seemed to her but a trifling one; she added:

"It has happened to me to behold something almost too shameful to relate, and this is that man seems to live quite merrily in sin; it astonishes me that a thing so terrible should receive so little consideration." She said again: "When I see and contemplate what God is, and what our own misery is, and behold the many ways by which he seeks to exalt us, I am transported beyond myself with astonishment. On the part of man, I see such a perversity and rebellion against God, that it seems impossible to bend his will except by the lure of things greater than those he enjoys here in this life. This is because the soul loves visible things, and will not renounce one but with the hope of four. And even with this hope, she would still seek to escape, if God did not retain her by his exterior and interior graces, without which man, whose instincts are naturally corrupt, could not be saved; for we are naturally corrupt, could not be saved; for we are naturally prone to add actual to original sin, and to continually tend toward earth for our satisfactions. And as Adam opposed his own will to the divine will, so we must seek to have the will of God as our only object, and by it to have our own disposed and annihilated. And as we cannot by ourselves discover our own evil inclinations, and our secret self-love, nor possibly annihilate our own self-will, it is very useful to subject our will to that of some other creature, and to do its bidding for the love of God. And the more we so subject ourselves for that divine love, so much the more shall we emancipate ourselves from that evil plague of our self-will which is so subtle and hidden within us, and works in so many ways, and defends itself by so many pleas that it is like the very demon. What it cannot effect in one way, it does in another, and this under many disguises. Now it is known as charity, now as necessity, justice, perfection, or suffering for God, or seeking for spiritual consolation, or for health, or as a good example to others, or a condescension to those who seek our advantage. It is an abyss, so deep and dangerous, that no one but God can save us from it. And as he sees this more clearly than we, he has great compassion for us, and never ceases to send us good inspirations and to seek to liberate us, not by forcing our free-will, but rather by disposing us in so many loving ways, that the soul, when she comes to understand the great care which God has taken of her, is forced to exclaim: 'O my God, it appears to me that thou hast nothing else to think of but my salvation! What am I that thou shouldst so care for me? Thou art God who thus carest for me, and I am nothing but myself. Can it be possible that I should not esteem what thou esteemest? that I should not remain ever obedient to thy commandments, and attentive to all the gracious inspirations thou sendest me by so many ways?'"

CHAPTER XIII

How she sees the source of goodness is in God, and how
creatures participate in it.

"I saw," said she, "a sight which greatly consoled me. I was shown the living source of goodness in God, as it was when yet alone and unparticipated in by any creature. Then I saw it begin to communicate itself to the creatures, and it did so to the fair company of angels, in order to give them the fruition of its own ineffable glory, demanding no other return from them than that they should recognize themselves as creatures, created by the supreme goodness, and having their being wholly from God, apart from whom all things are reduced to pure nonentity. The same must be said of the soul, which also was created immortal, that it might attain to beatitude; for if there were no immortality there could be no happiness. And because the angels were incapable of annihilation, therefore when their pride and disobedience robed them in the vesture of sin, God deprived them of that participation in his goodness, which, by his grace, he had ordained to give them: hence they remained so infernal and terrible that none, even of those who are specially enlightened by God, can possibly conceive their degradation. He did not, however, subtract all his mercy from them, for had he done so, they would be still more malicious, and would have a hell as infinitely immense in torture as it is in duration.

"God also is patient with man, his creature, while he remains in this world (although in sin), supporting him by his goodness, by which we are either tortured, or enabled to endure joyfully all grievous things, accordingly as he wishes to impart more or less to us. Of this goodness we sinners participate in this life, because God knows our flesh, which is the occasion of so much ignorance and weakness; and, therefore, while we are in this present life, he bears patiently with us, and allures us to him by hidden communications of his bounty: but, should we die in mortal sin (which God forbid), then he would deprive us of his mercy, and leave us to ourselves; yet not altogether so, because in every place he wills that his mercy shall accompany his justice. And were it possible to find a creature which in no degree participated in the divine goodness, it would be almost as bad as God is good.

"This I say, because God showed me somewhat of his truth, in order that I might know what man is without him; that is, when the soul is found in mortal sin, at that time, it is so monstrous and horrible to behold, that it is impossible to imagine anything equally so.

"No one need be surprised at this which I say and feel, namely, that I can no longer live in myself, that I am with a single motion of my own proper will, intellect, or memory. Wherefore, whether I speak, walk, remain quiet, sleep, eat, or do anything else, as if from my own proper self, I do not feel or know it. All these things are so far removed from me, that is, from the interior of my heart, that the distance is like that between heaven and earth; and if any of these things could by any mode enter into me, and give me such an enjoyment as ordinarily they produce, without doubt, I should be filled with misery, for I should feel it to be a retrogression from that which had formerly been shown me, and that it ought to have been destroyed. In this manner, all my natural inclinations, both of soul and body, are being consumed; and I know it to be necessary that all that is ours should waste away until nothing of it can be found; this is on account of its malignity, which nothing is able to overcome but the infinite goodness of God; and if it be not hidden and consumed, it will never be possible for us to be freed from this goad which is more than infernal, and which, so far as we are concerned, I behold to grow more horrible daily, so that one who was interiorly enlightened, yet had no confidence in God, would be driven to despair by the sight; so dreadful are

41

we when compared to God, who, with great love and solicitude, continually seeks to aid us."

It was still further shown to her in spirit how all the works of men (especially those which are spiritual), without the aid of supernatural grace, remain near God, without fruit, and are of little or no value. She saw also that God never fails to knock at the heart of man in order to enter therein and justify his works, and that none can ever complain that he was not called, for God is ever knocking, and not more at the hearts of the good than at those of the evil.

CHAPTER XIV

How she was entirely transformed in God, and hated to say me or mine.—What pride is.—Of the error of man who seeks for plenty and happiness on earth, where they cannot be found.— What a misfortune it is to be without love.

And continuing her discourse, she said: "I have always seen, and I am ever seeing more and more clearly, that there is no good except in God, and that all lesser goods which can be found are such only by participation; but pure and simple love cannot desire to receive from God anything, however good it may be, which is merely a good of participation, because God wishes it to be as pure, great, and simple as he is himself, and if the least thing were wanting to this perfection, love could not be contented, but would suffer as if in hell. And therefore I say that I cannot desire any created love, that is, love which can be felt, enjoyed, or understood. I do not wish love that can pass through the intellect, memory, or will; because pure love passes all these things and transcends them." She said also:

"I shall never rest until I am hidden and enclosed in that divine heart wherein all created forms are lost, and, so lost, remain thereafter all divine; nothing else can satisfy true, pure, and simple love. Therefore I have resolved so long as I live to say always to the world that it may do with my exterior as it wills, but with my interior this cannot be allowed, because it cannot, it will not occupy itself except in God, nor could it possibly wish to do otherwise, for he has locked it up within himself and will discover it to no one.

"Knowing that with all his power he is continually striving to annihilate this humanity, his creature, both inwardly and outwardly, in order that when it is entirely destroyed, the soul may issue with him from the body and thus united ascend to heaven; in my soul, therefore, I can see no one but God, since I suffer no one else to enter there, and myself less than any other, because I am my own worst enemy."

"If, however, it happens to be necessary to speak of myself, I do so on account of the world, which would not understand me should I name myself otherwise than as men are named, yet inwardly I say: my self is God, nor is any other self known to me except my God.

"And likewise when I speak of being, I say: all things which have being, have it from the essence of God by his participation: but pure love cannot stop to contemplate this general participation coming from God, nor to consider whether in itself, considered as a creature, it receives it in the same way as do the other creatures which more or less participate with God. Pure love cannot endure such comparison; on the contrary, it exclaims with a great impetus of love; my being is God, not by participation only but by a true transformation and annihilation of my proper being.

"Now take an example: the elements are not capable of transformation, for it is their nature to remain fixed, and, because this is the law of their being, they have not free-will, and it is impossible for them to vary from their original state. But every one who desires to remain firm in his own mind must have God as his chief end, who arrests every creature at that end for which he has created it, otherwise it would be impossible to detain it; it is insatiable until it has reached its true centre, which is God himself.

"Now although man is created for the possession of happiness, yet, having deviated from his true end, his nature has become deformed and is entirely repugnant to true beatitude. And on this account we are forced to submit to God this depraved nature of ours which fills our understanding with so many occupations, and causes us to deviate from the true path, in order that he may entirely consume it until nothing remains there but himself; otherwise the soul could never attain stability nor repose, for she was created for no other end.

"Therefore, whenever God can do so, he attracts the free-will of man by sweet allurements, and afterwards disposes it in such a manner that all things may conduce to the annihilation of man's proper being. So that in God is my being, my me, my strength, my beatitude, my good, and my delight. I say mine at present because it is not possible to speak otherwise; but I do not mean by it any such thing as me or mine, or delight or good, or strength or stability, or beatitude; nor could I possibly turn my eyes to behold such things in heaven or in earth; and if, notwithstanding, I sometimes use words which may have the likeness of humility and of spirituality, in my interior I do not understand them, I do not feel them. In truth it astonishes me that I speak at all, or use words so far removed from the truth and from that which I feel. I see clearly that man in this world deceives himself by admiring and esteeming things which are not, and neither sees nor esteems the things which are. Listen to what Fra Giacopone says about this in one of his lauds, that one which commences: O love of poverty. He says: What appears to thee, is not, so great is that which is; pride is in heaven; humility condemns itself. He says what appears, that is, all things visible and created are not and have no true being in themselves; so great is that which is, namely God, in whom is all true being. Pride is in heaven; that is, the true greatness is in heaven and not on earth; humility condemns itself, that is, the affections placed on things created which are humble and vile, not having in themselves any true being.

"But let us consider more attentively this matter namely this human blindness which takes white for black and holds pride for humility and humility for pride, and from which springs the perverse judgment which is the cause of all confusion. Let us see what pride may be. I say, according to what I see with the interior eye, pride is nothing else but an elevation of the mind to things which surpass man and are above his dignity, and whenever man abandons that which is, and which knows, and

45

which is powerful, for that which in truth has neither existence, knowledge, nor power, this is not pride.

"This degrades him, and it generates that pride accompanied by presumption, self-esteem, and arrogance which occasions so many sins against charity for the neighbor; for man believes himself to be such as he appears in his disordered mind which is so full of miseries. Therefore God says to this proud man: If thou seekest, according to the nature of the created soul, for such great things as seem at present to be good and for that happiness which belongs to earth, know that they are not, they cannot satisfy nor afford contentment seek rather in heaven, where pride is lawful, and where it is not placed in things empty and vain, but in those which are really great, which always remain and which cause a sinless pride; but if thou seekest after worthless things thou shalt never find them and shalt lost those which thou shouldst have sought.

"If man's eyes were pure, he would see clearly that things which pass away so quickly as do those which in this world are esteemed beautiful, good, and useful, could not truly be said to be so, such words being suitable only for things which have no end. Hence, man, if he prides himself upon temporal things, becomes unable to attain those that are celestial and eternal, degenerates into a vile and humble creature whose greatness is lost and who is degraded to the condition of the things he has always sought. Think, alas, what will become of this spirit so generous, created for the highest dignity and felicity, when it is immersed in the vile filth of its own depraved desires and held by its own demerits in abominations which will ever grow worse, but which will never end and which have no remedy? Alas! what pain, what anguish, and what desperate tears shall then be to this poor soul!

"We see and know by experience that only two causes could enable the spirit to remain in a place of torture: one of these is force, and the other the hope of a great reward for such endurance. What despair then will not man suffer when the force which detains him in hell shall never cease, and the pain shall have no remuneration? It is certain that our spirit was created for love and for felicity and this is what it is constantly seeking in all things; it can never find satiety in temporal things and yet is ever hoping that it may there attain it. Finally it deceives itself and loses that time which is so precious, and which was given it that it might seek God, the supreme good, in whom may be found the true love and the holy satisfaction which should be its true satiety and full repose. But what will it do in the end, when, having lost all its occupations, and discovered all its illusions and its vain hopes, and lost all its time, it remains deprived of every good, and, though contrary to its nature, must forever remain forcibly deprived of all love and felicity? This one thing alone is so painful and terrible to contemplate that to speak of it makes me tremble with fear.

"By this I comprehend what hell and heaven may be, because, as I see that man by love becomes one with God, in whom he finds all happiness, so, on the contrary I see that, deprived of love he remains as full of woes as he would have of joys (and that is infinitely) if he had not been so mad. Therefore, although we hear it said that hell is a great punishment, yet this does not appear to me to express it, nor can its gravity be truly told or comprehended, neither could it be represented to one as I understand it; only by the greatness of love in, the true and omnipotent God, can that which is opposed to it be measured.

"When I consider the blindness of those who, for the sake of things so vile and little, allow themselves to be stupidly led away into the abyss of such horrible and infinite woe, all that is within me is moved by a great compassion. In this connection I recall a possessed person who was forced by a religious to declare who he was: he cried out with great force: 'I am that wretch who is deprived of love.' He said this with a voice so piteous and penetrating that inwardly I was filled with pity, especially when I was hearing those words, Deprived of love."

47

CHAPTER XV

How contrary to pure love is even the slightest imperfection.—
Of the many means by which God ministers to our salvation.—At
the point of death we shall esteem the opposition made to the
divine inspirations as worse than hell itself.

"I see clearly," said our saint, "that when pure love sees even
the least imperfection in man, if the mercy of God did not
sustain it, it would grind into powder not only the body, but even
the soul itself, were it not immortal, knowing that so long as it is
retained he must be deprived of love. I see that the cause of all
these evils is that we are so blinded by the enormity of our sins
that it is impossible to comprehend, as we should, the extremity
of our misery, which is yet supremely necessary for us to know.
When man is reduced to his last agony—and in that hour all joys
flee from him and all evils present themselves without a
remedy—I cannot find words to express the great pain and
anguish which will then overwhelm his soul, and therefore I am
silent.

"O unhappy man, in that hour wilt see how much more
solicitous God has been for thy salvation than thou hast been
thyself! Then thy whole life will pass before thine eyes, with all
its opportunities for well-doing and all its rejected inspirations,
and in one instant thou wilt clearly see the whole. Believest thou
that thy soul must still live when it passes from such injustice
into the presence of true justice? It is not possible for me to
dwell upon this thought, for I find it so painful; I am constrained
to cry out, Beware, beware, for the matter is of such infinite
importance. If I thought I should be understood I would never
say aught else. When I see men die as the beasts die, without
fear, without light, without grace, and know how serious a thing

this is, I should suffer for my neighbor the greatest pains that I could ever feel, if God did not sustain me. And when I hear it said that God is good and he will pardon us, and then see that men cease not from evil-doing, oh, how it grieves me! The infinite goodness with which God communicates with us, sinners as we are, should constantly make us love and serve him better; but we, on the contrary, instead of seeing in his goodness an obligation to please him, convert it into an excuse for sin which will of a certainty lead in the end to our deeper condemnation.

"I see that God, so long as man remains in this life, uses all the ways of mercy for his salvation, and gives him all the graces necessary to that end, like a benignant and most clement father who knows only how to do us good; and especially he does so in enduring our sins, which in his sight are so very great that if unsustained by his goodness, man would be ground into powder by them.

"But man does not comprehend this, and God graciously awaits and bears with him until his death; then he resorts to justice, although not even then is it unmixed with mercy, since in hell man does not suffer according to his deserts, yet woe be to him who falls therein, for truly he suffers greatly. And when I see man fix his affections on creatures, even, as he sometimes does, on a dog or a cat, or any other created thing, delighting greatly in it, doing all that he can to serve it, unable to admit into his heart any other love, and as it were, breathing by it, I long to exterminate these things which hold him thus employed and cause him to lose the great reward of the love of God which alone can satisfy and make him happy.

"Alas, this one word I will say about the just and holy ordinance of God, although I know not whether it will be understood. God has ordained man for beatitude, and that with more love than can possible be conceived, and all proper means to this result he gives him with infinite charity, perfection, and purity, so that man does not lose the least atom that is justly his; and, notwithstanding how many sins he may have committed,

God never ceases to send him all needful inspirations, admonitions, and chastisements to lead him to that degree of happiness for which he created him with such heartfelt love. And he does this in such a way that when man shall behold it after his death, he will well understand that he never suffered himself to be led by the divine goodness, and that he has lost God solely through his own fault. Then the opposition he has made to such divine goodness will torture him more than hell itself; because all the pains of hell, however great they may be, are as nothing in comparison to the privation of the beatific vision which is caused by their own resistance.

"This is proved by divine love, which says that it esteems the smallest imperfection a greater evil than any hell that can be imagined. What, then, shall be said of that soul which in all things finds itself opposed to the divine ordinations, except that infinite woe awaits it, infinite tribulations, dolors, and afflictions, without remedy, without consolation, and without end, and that it shall be plunged in profound humiliation and infernal gloom."

CHAPTER XVI

That she understood her own nothingness, and therefore would not speak about herself.—Of her great faith in God.—How willful and malicious we are in ourselves, and how necessary it is to abandon all to God.

So great was the humility of this holy soul that she saw her own nothingness most clearly, and would never speak of herself, neither well nor ill. She said:

"As to the evil, I know well that is all my own, the good I could not possibly do of myself, for nothing cannot produce something." Nor would she speak, as is customary, of being wicked, lest her lower nature might grow confident and presume upon the knowledge of its incapacity for good: and having such an opinion of herself, instead of desiring the esteem of others, she cut away even the root of presumption, saying:

"I will never say anything about myself, either good or bad, lest I should come to esteem myself of some importance: and when I have sometimes heard myself spoken of by others, especially if I were praised, I have said inwardly: 'If you knew what I am within, you would not speak thus.' And then, turning to myself, I say: 'When thou hearest thyself named, or listenest to words which perhaps may seem to praise thee, know that they are not spoken of what is thine; for the only virtue and glory thou hast belong to God, and thou hast at least in thine earthly and carnal nature no more conformity with good than has the demon; but when evil is spoken of thee, remember that all could not be said which is in reality true; thou art unworthy even to be called worthless, because to speak of thee at all lends thee a fictitious value.'"

Hence, knowing herself, all the confidence of this great soul was in God, in whom she was so grounded and established that it was hardly to be called faith, for she saw herself more secure in the hands of God, her Love, than if she were actually in possession of all the goods and felicities which it is possible to desire or to think of having in this world; and having placed all her trust in God, and given him full control of her, she covered herself under the mantle of his providential care.

She became such an enemy to herself that nothing but necessity ever caused her to speak of herself at all, and she would never do so in particular but would generally say us; and she said: "The evil nature of man is pleased with being mentioned, and the greatest blow that can be given it is never to speak of it at all, and never make it of any account; therefore do not willingly name it in any manner." And to her own nature she said: "I know thee and rate thee as thou deservest: thou canst not advocate thy cause with me." And if an angel had come to say a word in favor of herself, she would not have believed him, so certain was she of her own malignity.

And, having this clear knowledge of herself, she was constrained by it to accept with resignation whatever might befall either her body or her soul, so that whenever she found in herself any defect or any pain, she would say quickly: "These things are caused solely by my own evil nature, and of this I am so certain that I know not how I could produce other fruits than these which are so hateful. I never could do so if God did not assist me. But I know well, having been shown by God the imperfections and malignity of our own inclination, that we can never, except by the help of divine grace, do anything but evil. Good is as hopeless to us as to the demons, and even more so, for, unlike them, we have a body and a free-will which ally themselves to our depravity and do all the evil they can, which is more or less accordingly as God abandons us to our own control.

"But, for one who desires to approach God, it is necessary to become the enemy of his enemies; and, as I find nothing that is worse than myself, nor that is more inimical to him, I am compelled to hold myself in more aversion than anything else whatever, and will even despise myself and count it to be worthless. And, on the other hand, I will detach my spirit from all the goods of both this world and the other, which I will henceforth regard as if they had no existence. I have implored God neither to suffer me to rejoice interiorly nor to grieve over any created thing, so that I may never be seen to shed a single tear. And I have begged him to take away from me the freedom of my will, so that I may no longer do what pleases me, but only what is according to his pleasure: all these things I have obtained from his clemency.

"Now, seeing me thus determined, my self said to me: 'Grant me, at least, the consolation of not hearing myself thus spoken of: for, whatever I am, it is necessary that I should exist in some manner. There is no creature which is not suitably provided for according to its needs, and I also am one of God's creatures.' Then the spirit rose up and answered: Thou art indeed a creature of God, but thou art not according to God, and if thou wishest to be so thou must be first despoiled of all thou hast previously acquired, first by original sin and afterwards by the actual sins which thou hast freely multiplied, and which are more odious in the sight of God than thou couldst believe were it told thee. And when I see thee more covered with secret sins than a cat is with hairs, I know not where thou findest courage to say that thou art of God. If I were so mad as to feed thee according to thy inclinations, which are so corrupt and contrary to the purity which God requires, I should do two evil and perilous things: one is that I should never satisfy thee, and the other that thou wouldst every day grow stronger and wound me more and more acutely; and as I am myself full of evil, thou wouldst attack me secretly and in an apparently spiritual manner, and then no one but God could overcome thee. Speak to me no more of thy crafty designs, for I have determined to disregard thee.

"Recommend thyself to God that he may aid thee, and I also will assist thee by his help. Moreover, I will pray him to consume all thy perverse inclinations and to restore thee again to that primitive innocence in which he created thee, for otherwise thou canst never be satisfied: no one can satiate thee but he who created thee and who alone knows all thy secret desires and can grant them without difficulty. Cease, then, to seek for other satisfactions, for however abundant may be thy possessions thou wilt still remain poor and in want; when once thou art justified, all will be given thee which heaven and earth can afford.

"Know then that I despise thee and would rather choose to be condemned to hell without thee, than to possess God through thy means. For a pure mind cannot suffer anything to come between itself and God, for it desires to possess him entirely and to be as pure and simple as he is himself. And this being so, how could it endure to be assisted by thee who art so hideous, and who would always glorify thyself unworthily over thy achievements? And although I know that such a thing could never be, it fills me with indignation to find that I have even imagined it or that any mind should ever conceive it possible!

"Thus scorned, my self knew not what to answer, and never more had courage to assert itself: it no longer looked either at the body or the soul, toward heaven or toward earth; but I saw it remain always by itself with all its malicious inclinations, and had God permitted it, it would have done more evil against him than Lucifer himself. Yet, as I saw that God continually restrained it, this sight gave me no uneasiness, nor did it ever cause me any torment or suffering. Rather was the effect directly contrary, for he who loves justice is rejoiced when robbers are punished, and surely he who, being evil by nature, desires to become good by his own efforts, is a robber worthy to be punished in hell-fire.

"Hence, when I saw its malignant inclinations entirely subjected to God and by him executed and annihilated, I was greatly contented, and the more clearly I saw my own proper wickedness, so much the greater pleasure did I take in his justice. And truly, it appears to me that if I could fear anything it would be my own self—which is utterly evil; yet when I saw it in the hands of God I abandoned it to him with confidence, and never since then have I felt any fear concerning it; rather, I may say, that I never think about it and make no more account of it than if it in no way concerned me.

"I saw others weeping over their perversities and their evil desires, and forcing themselves to resist them; yet, the more they strove to remedy their defects the more often did they fall. And when any one spoke of this to me, I answered You have woes and you weep over them, and I have them and I do not weep. You do evil and you lament, and I should do the same if the almighty God did not assist me. You cannot defend yourself, nor can I do so either; hence it is necessary that we should yield ourselves to him who only can deliver us from evil, and he will do for us what is wholly beyond our power. And in this way we shall find rest from this our evil self, which is always torturing itself to its own destruction: yet when it is imprisoned by God, it remains submissive and in silence."

CHAPTER XVII

In what manner God deals with one who corresponds with him.—And how the saint abhorred spiritual delights, and how God cast around her the chain of pure love.

This holy woman said that when God disposes a soul to correspond to him with her free will by placing herself wholly in his hands, he leads her to every perfection; thus has he dealt with one who, after she was thus called, never more followed her own will, but always stood waiting interiorly upon the will of God, which she so confidently felt to be impressed upon her mind that she sometimes said to him: "In all that I think, speak, or do, I trust in thee that thou wilt not permit me to offend thee."

The following rule with regard to the intellect was given to this soul, namely: never to attempt to understand anything in heaven or on earth and, least of all, the spiritual operations in her self; and she obeyed so implicitly that she never more observed curiously anything in herself or in others.

If it were asked in what manner the intellectual powers were employed, I should answer that all the powers of the soul were always under the command and in the service of God, and when anything had to be done, at that instant, and in so far as necessity required, it was given her to know what she should do, and then the door was closed.

Of the memory she could give no account, for it seemed as if she were without memory and without intellect. This was not caused by any voluntary act of hers, but was the result of seeing herself so often and so suddenly moved to action, that she easily comprehended that it was God who was operating in her, and she remained occupied in him, and lost to all sense of time or place and without the will or the ability to do otherwise, except when God suddenly effected some change in her. Nor was she ever able to consider anything except what God at the moment proposed to her; in this manner she was attentive to whatever she was doing so long as necessity required, but when it was finished all memory of it passed with it.

The same thing was true of her affections, which were taken from her by her Love even at the beginning, and in such a way that she could no longer love anything created or uncreated, not even God himself, at least as he was revealed in those sentiments, in visions, delights, and spiritual correspondences which all others who beheld them estimated so highly, but which she on the contrary held in horror and sought to fly from. But the more she sought to avoid them the more were they given to her, and they increased in such a manner that her body was often entirely prostrated by them. Her soul, however, remained pure and serene, as if it were passed beyond such violence, and were filled with divine sweetness. And when this was over, she seemed to be improved both in mind and body. Yet she had no desire for such improvement, and sought for nothing but God, her Love, in comparison with whom she rejected all, even that which proceeded from him, as being of less value, or indeed as nothing.

This integrity of the will she held so cautiously and was always so hidden in God that no illusion, imagination or inspiration could interpose between them, nor even any truth which was not immediately from him.

Therefore when God took from her the burden and the care of herself, her spirit found itself all light and able to do great things, and the instinct of love which God gave it when it was thus separated from her proper self, was so swift and great and powerful that she could satisfy it nowhere but in God. Then God, seeing her so disposed and well prepared, cast down from heaven one end of the cord of his most upright, pure, and holy love, and with it held her so closely occupied in him that she readily understood that she sprang from him and corresponded with him. Yet, in all this her humanity had no share, and neither felt, saw nor understood it.

Thus she allowed this clear water to flow descending as from a living fountain; and by means of her love and of her great purity she saw every little defect which to her appeared offensive: and if it had been possible for her to tell the great importance of every least impediment to the divine love, even hearts of adamant would have been ground into powder by fear of them.

CHAPTER XVIII

How she did not desire love for God or in God, nor to have any medium between herself and God.—She could not see how love could be increased in her.—Of the peace of the soul transformed in God.

This holy Soul said that she never spoke of these great things to others without its appearing to her afterwards that she had told a lie—so weak were her words in comparison with that which she experienced through her pure and upright love. She said, therefore: "I do not wish a love which may be described as for God, or in God. I cannot see those words, for and in, without their suggesting to me that something may intervene between God and me; and that is what pure and simple love, by reason of its purity and simplicity, is unable to endure. This purity and simplicity is as great as God is, for it is his own." At another time she said that she never felt like speaking of this simplicity and purity of love, as if she had a sensible experience of it, because it is entirely ineffable and above the capacity of man; yet she had it in such abundance that, whatever might be alleged or even proved to the contrary, she could not understand how it could increase within her. This must be understood to mean that, being always replenished with love, she could neither see nor desire more than that which at any moment held her satisfied; this, however, did not prevent love from continually purifying and cleansing this precious and elect vessel, and from ever increasing and more abundantly filling her.

And to prove this, she said: "Every day I felt myself lifted above those trifles which this pure love, ever harassing itself with those penetrating eyes that behold even those smallest imperfections which to other love appear perfection, was striving to cast out. This work is done by God, and man himself is not aware of it, nor does he see these imperfections; on the contrary, because such a sight would be insupportable to him, God shows him the perfected work as if it were without a flaw. Yet God does not cease continually to purify him, although he does it in a way not comprehensible to any intellect. It is written that even the heavens are not pure in the sight of God, by which it must be understood that such purity is not known, except by the help of a supernatural light which, without any assistance from man, works in him after its own pleasure, and ever cleanses him more fully until he is entirely pure. And this work God does secretly, because, when man yields himself wholly into the hands of God (which without divine grace he is unable even to wish to do), he can then see the enormity of even one trifling imperfection in the sight of God; and afterward, if he could see all those defects in himself which God is daily removing from him, he would be overpowered by his despair. Hence it is that these obstacles are gradually removed without man's cognizance, and God continually operates in us by his sweet goodness so long as we remain in this present life."

When the good God calls us in this world, he finds us full of vices and sins, and his first work is to give us the instinct to practice virtue; then he incites us to desire perfection, and afterwards, by infused grace, he conducts us to the true annihilation, and finally to the true transformation. This is the extraordinary road along which God conducts the soul. But when the soul is thus annihilated and transformed, it no longer works, or speaks, or wills, or feels, or understands, nor has it in itself any knowledge, either of that which is internal or external, which could possibly affect it; and, in all these things God is its director and guide without the help of any creature.

In this state, the soul is in such peace and tranquility that it seems to her that both soul and body are immersed in a sea of the profoundest peace, from which she would not issue for anything that could happen in this life. She remains immovable, imperturbable, and neither her humanity nor her spirit feels anything except the sweetest peace, of which she is so full, that if her flesh, her bones, her nerves were pressed, nothing would issue from them but peace. And all day long she sings softly to herself for joy, saying: "Shall I show thee what God is? No one finds peace apart from him."

And as this process goes on, she is every day more profoundly plunged, immersed, and transformed in this peace, so that her humanity is every day more alienated from the world and from all things earthly and natural; and this in such wise that even the body no longer lives upon corporal food, and yet neither wastes away nor dies; on the contrary, this creature remains in health without using the means which are the cause of health, because it is no longer supported by nature but by an incomprehensible satiety which overflows into the body. And this is doubtless the reason why such a creature becomes so marvelous in her aspect, and especially in her purified eyes, which are like two ardent stars, enkindled in heaven, so that she appears truly like an angel upon earth.

This love is of so generous and excellent a spirit that it disdains to lose its time in anything, however beautiful and precious, except its own purity and splendor, from which issue translucent rays of ardent and inflamed virtue. Thus is she ever occupied, and all things else she esteems as no longer appertaining to her.

This work is constantly progressing, and every day the soul understands more clearly that the end for which man was created was truly for love, and to delight himself in this pure and holy love. And therefore when man has, by the assistance of divine grace, arrived at this desired port of pure love, he can afterwards do nothing (even if he wished or tried to force himself to do otherwise) but love and enjoy himself: this grace God gives to man in a manner so admirable and above every human desire or comprehension that without doubt, being still in this present life, he feels himself to have been made a partaker of the beatific glory.

CHAPTER XIX

Of her earnest answer to a Friar Preacher who told her how much better he was prepared than herself for the divine love.— Nothing can hinder divine love, neither can it be deceived.—Also of its various conditions.

On one occasion a friar preacher, either to try her, or under some wrong impression, as often happens, maintained that he was better prepared for the divine love than herself, alleging as a reason, that on entering religion, he had renounced everything external and internal, and therefore he was more free and better prepared to love God than herself; and for many other reasons such as men can adduce, who are more learned than holy and devout, but especially because she was wedded to the world, and himself to religion.

When the friar had said many things of this kind, an ardent flame of pure love seized the blessed Catherine, with which her heart was so inflamed, that she rose to her feet and fervently exclaimed: "If I believed that your habit would add one spark to my love, I would not hesitate to tear it from you, if I could obtain it in no other way. Whatever you merit more than I, through the renunciation you have made for God's sake, and through your religious life, which continually enables you to merit, I do not seek to obtain; these are yours; but that I cannot love God as much as yourself, you can never make me believe."

She uttered these words with so much fervor and effect, that her hair burst from the band that confined it, and fell disheveled over her shoulders, so that, in her burning zeal, she seemed almost beside herself; and yet so graceful and decorous was her bearing, that all persons present were amazed, edified, and pleased; and she added: Love cannot be checked, and if checked it is not pure and simple love."

When she reached the house, she said, after the manner in which she was accustomed to speak familiarly with her Lord: "O Love, who shall prevent me from loving thee? not only in the world as I am" (meaning the married state), "but even if I should find myself in a camp of soldiers, I could not be prevented from loving thee. If the world, or if the husband could impede love, what would such love be but a thing of feeble virtue and mean capacity? As for me I know by what I have experienced that divine love can be conquered or impeded by nothing. It conquers all things."

Catherine did not intend to say that the path to perfect love was as easy to seculars as to religious: but what she said applied only to perfect and pure love; because such a love breaks through all restraints and conquers all difficulties.

On being told that she might be deceived by the devil, she replied: "I cannot believe that a love which has nothing of self in it can ever be deceived." And God communicated to her interiorly, that she was in the right, saying to her, that if it were possible for one to love even the devil with pure love, free from everything pertaining to self, malignant and odious as he is, he could not harm this soul, for pure love has such virtue that it would deprive him of his malignity. If, then, pure love has such power over one so wicked, who can doubt of a soul who possesses it? For if pure and simple love in any creature could be deceived, God cannot be.

Catherine being on one occasion greatly troubled and oppressed by her humanity, because she had consented, in order to sustain a feeble and infirm life, to use things lawful and permitted, God thus instructed her concerning these things: "I never wish you to turn your eyes towards anything but love, and there rest, unmoved by any novelty that may present itself, within and without, but be like one dead to all things; because he who trusts in me must never doubt himself. For all the reasoning, cogitations, alternations, and doubts, which man has concerning the spirit, proceed from that very evil root of self, for pure love transcends all human thoughts, and will not live in the soul, still less in the body of man according to their nature, but will do all things above the capacity of that nature, and all that it thinks and speaks is always above nature."

CHAPTER XX

That God does not wish man to serve him through self-interest or through fear, but only through faith and love, and therefore he sweetly attracts his will.—The saint did not desire grace or mercy, but only justice.—That pure love fears nothing but sin.

This holy Soul being (as may be inferred from what has been already said) arrived at that state of perfection where she began to taste the fruition of eternal happiness, and regarding those who are still deceived by the passions of the present time, and know not how to hasten from that which is so wholly evil, was moved by compassion, and she said:

"O man, created in such great dignity, why dost thou lose thyself in things so vile? If thou shouldst consider well, thou wouldst easily see that all worldly things which thou desirest are as nothing when compared to those spiritual goods which God gives thee even in this life, which is so full of ignorance. Pray that thou mayst come hereafter to that celestial country in which are things which eye hath not seen nor ear heard, neither hath it entered into the heart of man to conceive what God hath prepared for them that love him!"

If man clearly saw that by well-doing he could gain eternal life, and could imagine how great the happiness of heaven will be, he would always persevere in good; and even should he live until the end of the world, he would never occupy his memory, intellect, or will on any but celestial things. But God wishes that faith should be meritorious, and not that man should serve him through self-interest; and therefore he conducts him by degrees, although he always gives him sufficient knowledge to support his faith. But afterwards he gives him such aforetaste of eternal glory, that by a clear and certain perception which he receives at the close of this life, the faith of the man, thus replenished with heavenly delights almost ceases to be faith.

On the other hand, if man could know how greatly he must suffer hereafter for his sins, hold it for certain that for very fear he would not only abandon all things, but that he would not commit the smallest sin. But God does not wish to be served through fear, because, if man's heart were filled with terror, love could find no entrance there. It is through love that God does not permit man to behold this dreadful sight, although he does in part discover it to those who are so protected and occupied with that pure love which casteth out fear that the doors cannot be shut against them. These souls see in heaven and earth things which tongue cannot express, and they are drawn by sweet allurements and gentle ways. This is what happens to those who allow themselves to be led by faith, and who, recognizing the benignant hand of God in all that befalls them, never reject it, but rather cleave to it strongly and follow it with joy.

But those who refuse so much goodness and deliberately persevere in living according to their own desires, will have at the moment of their death a vision so painful and so terrible, that, having in themselves even one defect, they will be unable to endure the sight. And, therefore amazed at such stupidity, the saint exclaimed: "O miserable man, who will not provide against a fate so unhappy, and caused only by thine own obstinacy! Thou thinkest not of it, yet know that it will befall thee when it is too late. In heaven nothing can enter which is defiled, and purgatory must cleanse thee before thou canst attain eternal felicity."

"God," she said, "leads man by a road intermediate between these two. He shows him always great tokens of his love, in order to attract man, who is naturally more inclined to act through love than fear. Yet he gives him also the motive of fear, that by it he may more readily abandon his sins. But neither the love nor the fear which God grants him are so great as to force man towards him, because it is his will that grace should be accomplished by free-will and faith, by which man does all that is within his power. The rest God effects by his good inspirations, which, when once man has yielded his consent, easily incite him to combat his rebellious nature, and, by the help of the great satisfaction which God imparts, to hold it at its true value."

And therefore she said: "When I see that God is ever ready to give us all the interior and exterior aids necessary for our salvation, and that he observes our deeds solely for our own good; when, on the other hand, I see man continually occupied in useless things, contrary to himself and of no value; and that at the hour of death God will say to him: 'What is there, O man, that I could have done for thee which I have not done?' and that man will clearly know this to be true; I believe that he will have to render a stricter account for this than for all other sins, and I am amazed and cannot understand how man can be so mad as to neglect a thing of such vast and extreme importance."

The vision which she had of all this was not represented to her mind in a manner so weak as that in which it is here recounted, but so clearly that it seemed to her that she could see and touch it. And doubtless he who should behold such a sight would rather choose death itself than offend God voluntarily, even in the least degree. This, however, did not cause her such wonder when she considered the great evils from which men are freed and the eternal joys to which they are destined and sweetly guided. Therefore she held herself in great aversion and did not hesitate to say: "In this life I desire neither grace nor mercy, but only justice and vengeance upon the evil-doer." She said this with much earnestness, because she saw that the mercy and goodness of God toward his elect infinitely surpass their gratitude toward him and their sorrow for their sins, and therefore she could not endure that her own offences against her Love should go unpunished.

This appeared to be the reason why she cared little about gaining plenary indulgences; not that she did not hold them in great reverence and devotion, or esteem them of great value, but that for her own part she would rather be chastised and receive the just punishment assigned her, than by this satisfaction be released in the sight of God. The Offended seemed to her to be of such goodness, and the offender so much opposed to him in all things, that she could not endure to see anything which was not subjected to the divine justice, that so it might be well chastised. And, therefore, to abandon all hope of escaping this righteous pain she did not seek for plenary indulgences nor even recommend herself to the prayers of others, in order that she might be ever subject, and be punished and condemned as she had deserved.

What has just been said can be comprehended in the state of perfection to which the saint had been raised, and in which, being as it were secure of victory, she desired to combat purely for the greater glory of her Lord, and, like a valiant soldier, neither sought for nor desired any assistance. And being unable to support the sight of an offence against God, she said to him:

"My Love, I can endure all things else, but to have offended thee is a thing so dreadful and unbearable to me that I pray thee to let me suffer anything else than to see that I have done so. The insults that I have offered thee I am sorry to have offered, nor can I ever consent to offend thee more. At the hour of death show me rather all the demons with all their plains, for I would think it nothing in comparison with the sight of one offense against thee, however slight; though nothing could be slight which displeased thine infinite majesty.

"I know for certain that if the soul which truly loves, should behold in herself one thing which separated her from God, her Spouse, her body would be ground into powder. This I know by means of the extreme and unspeakable torments which I suffer from the interior fire which burns within me; and hence, I conclude that love cannot endure even the least opposition, nor will it remain with any one who does not first remove all obstacles and impediments in order to remain with it in peace and perfect quiet."

Chapter XXI

How she was disposed toward God and toward her neighbor.—
What pure and simple love is.

This holy Soul was so regulated by God, that in all that was
necessary and reasonable she satisfied every one; and although
she was entirely employed in serving her sweet Love, yet she
was never willing to displease her neighbor either in word or
deed, but on the contrary always assisted him as far as she was
able. She said, however, to her Lord: "Thou hast commanded me
to love my neighbor, and I am unable to love any one but thee,
or to admit any partner with thee: how then shall I obey thee?"
And interiorly he responded thus: "He who loves me loves also
all whom I love. It suffices that for the welfare of the neighbor
thou shouldst do all that is necessary for his soul and body. Such
a love as this is sure to be without passion; because it is not in
himself but in God that the neighbor should be loved."

Speaking afterwards on this subject, she said: "Before God
created man, love was pure and simple, free from all taint of
self-interest, and needing no restraint. And in creating man, God
was moved by no other cause except his pure love. In all that he
did for him he had no other motive or object. And as his love
allows nothing to prevent it from doing all possible good to its
beloved, and attends to nothing which is not necessary to that
end, so the love of man should return to God all that it receives
from him; and then, having no respect to anything but love, it
will fear nothing, because it never seeks its own advantage."

She said again: "Not only is pure love incapable of suffering,
but it cannot even comprehend what suffering or pain can be,
nor understand the wicked actions which it sees others do. And,
were it possible for it to feel all the pains which are felt by the

devils and the damned souls, it could never say that they were pains; because, in order to feel or comprehend pain, it truly is necessary to be without this love.

"The true and pure love is of such force that it cannot be diverted from its object, nor can it see or feel anything else. Hence it is useless toil to try to make such creatures employ themselves in the things of this world, for with regard to them they are as insensible as if they were dead.

"It is impossible to describe this love in words or figures which will not, in comparison with the reality, seem entirely false. This only can be understood, namely, that the human intellect is unable to comprehend it. And to him who seeks to know what it is that I know and feel, I can only reply that it transcends all utterance."

CHAPTER XXII

Of her vocation, which was like that of St. Paul.—That she was freed from suffering by her great love.—How terrible is man without grace.—How great is the stain of even one slight defect, and still more that of a sin.

The vocation and the correspondence of this holy Soul were like those of the glorious apostle St. Paul; that is, that in one instant (as was narrated in the beginning), she was made perfect. And this was evident, because in that instant and ever thereafter she proceeded not like a beginner but like one already perfect; for this reason she never knew how to give any account of the way to obtain perfection, because she herself had never attained it by acquired virtues, but simply by infused grace, which instantaneously wrought in her such effects as usually require the uninterrupted exercises of a whole life.

And being thus transformed in God, the fire of love which burned in her purified heart was as great at the beginning as at the end of her conversion—which was a miraculous thing. She said that after she was called and wounded with love she never experienced any suffering, either interior or exterior, either from the world, the devil, or the flesh, or from any other cause. This was the effect of her interior transformation in God, so that although many adversities befell her, nevertheless she never found her will opposed to them, but on the contrary she received all things as from God, and, thus mingled with his love, nothing failed to please her. Her humanity, too, was so subjected to the spirit that it never rebelled, although it was obliged to perform many penances; so that in her was fulfilled that saying: My heart and my flesh have rejoiced in the living God (Psalm lxxxiii).

And therefore she said: "When I see the greatness of the spiritual operation, and behold how important is any offence against God or his grace, I find it impossible to conceive of any other suffering or any other hell, than to have sinned against him. All other pains which it is possible to endure in this life, are consolations in comparison with this; just as, on the other hand, all things inferior to God which may seem to have a sort of goodness are yet, in comparison with him, only evil; this however, I know well, will hardly be understood by him who does not know it by experience.

"On the other hand, I know not how man can be so blind as not to see that unless God sustains us by his grace, we are full of sorrow, bitterness, wrath, discontent, and woe, even in this present life, where, however, we are never entirely abandoned by him, no matter how great our sins may be. For, if a man could possibly live this mortal life, when entirely forsaken by God (excepting only the divine justice, failing which he would be annihilated,) I am certain that whoever beheld such a being would die. And not only he who beheld him, but he who, though far removed from him, should learn of his existence and comprehend the misery of his state, would also be deprived of life. To be abandoned by God is a thing too terrible and vast for human words to express, or human intellects to comprehend.

"Alas! with how many perils is man surrounded in this life! When I consider of what great importance are spiritual life and death, if God did not sustain me I believe that I should die. If I could have any desire, it would be that of expressing all that I feel and know concerning this; and if it were granted me to demonstrate what I wish by martyrdom, I do not believe I could find any torments which I would not joyfully undergo, if so I might warn man of the importance of this truth.

"When I beheld that vision in which I saw the magnitude of the stain of even one least sin against God, I know not why I did not die. I said: 'I no longer marvel that hell is so horrible, since it was made for sin; for even hell (as I have seen it) I do not believe to be really proportionate to the dreadfulness of sin; on the contrary, it seems to me that even in hell God is very merciful, since I have beheld the terrible stain caused by but one venial sin. And what, in comparison to that, would be a mortal sin? And then so many mortal sins? Surely, if any one could behold all this, even if he were immortal, anguish would once more make him mortal. Even that slight and solitary vision which I beheld, and which lasted but an instant, if it had continued but a little longer would have destroyed my body had it been made of adamant.'

"But all that I can say concerning it seems false beside what I truly comprehend. For this vision brought me so near death that my blood congealed and my whole body was so enfeebled that I seemed to be passing beyond this life; but the goodness of God desired that I should live to narrate it.

"And afterwards I said: 'I no longer wonder that purgatory is as terrible as hell, since one is to punish and the other to cleanse: both of them are made for sin, which is so horrible that both its punishment and its purgation must needs correspond with it in horror.' Man could understand this if he considered his evil inclinations, and how wretched he is when left to himself. But God does not permit this vision to be seen except by those who are, as it were, confirmed in grace, and even these he allows to see only so much as will be for their own good and that of others. And he shows them also that goodness which rescues man from these great and incomprehensible perils to which he is subject,, although he beholds them not; but God knows them and their importance, and therefore the great love he bears us moves him to compassion, and so long as we are in this life he never ceases to incite us to well-doing, in order that we may not be more deeply plunged into evil."

From this may be seen how it was that the conversion of this Soul was accomplished, like that of St. Paul, who, rapt into heaven, beheld the glory of the just, while St. Catherine beheld the pains which sinners have merited by their crimes, how full of abomination they are, and how earnestly to be fled from.

Chapter XXIII

Of self-love and of divine love, and of their conditions.

This illuminated Soul said that she saw a vision of self-love, and beheld that its master and lord was the demon; and she said that self-hate would be a better name for it, because it makes man do all the evil that it wills, and in the end precipitates him into hell. She beheld it in man, as it were by essence, both spiritually and corporally, and in each of these ways it seemed so entirely incorporated with him that it appeared to her almost impossible that he should be purified in this life.

She said also: "The true self-love has these properties: First, it cares not whether it injures either its own soul and body or those of its neighbor, nor does it value the goods and reputation of either itself or others; for the sake of accomplishing its ends it is as rigorous with itself as with others, and will submit to no possible contradiction. When it has resolved upon any action, it remains unmoved by either promises or threats, how great soever they may be, but perseveres in its course, caring neither for slavery nor poverty, for infamy nor weakness, for purgatory, death, nor hell, for it is so blind that it cannot see these things or recognize their importance. If one should say to man that if he would abandon his self-love he would acquire riches, gain health, possess in this world all that heart can desire, and be certain of heaven hereafter, he would yet repel them all, because his heart is unable to value any good, either temporal or eternal, which does not bear the impress of self-love; everything else he despises and counts for nothing, while to this he becomes a slave, going wherever it wills, and so submissive that he has no other choice. He neither speaks, thinks, nor understands aught else. If he is called mad and foolish, he cares nothing for it, nor is he offended by the derision or others. He has shut his eyes and closed his ears to all else, and holds them as if they were not."

She said moreover: "Self-love is so subtle a robber that it commits its thefts, even upon God himself, without fear or shame, employing his goods as if they were its own, and assigning as a reason that it cannot live without them. And this robbery is hidden under so many veils of apparent good that it can hardly be detected except by the penetrating light of true love, which always desires to remain uncovered and bare, both in heaven and earth, because it has nothing shameful to conceal.

"And, therefore, self-love never understands the nature of pure love; for pure love sees not how the things which it knows as they are in truth could possibly be possessed or appropriated; nothing would displease it so much as to find anything which it could call its own; the reason of this is that pure love sees not, nor can it ever see, anything but truth itself, which, being by its nature communicable to all, can never be monopolized by any. Self-love, on the other hand, is in itself an obstacle to truth, and neither believes it nor beholds it, but rather, confiding in itself, holds truth as an enemy and an alien.

"But the spiritual self-love is much more perilous than the corporal, for it is bitter poison whose antidote is hard to find. It is yet more artfully veiled, and passes sometimes as sanctity or necessity, or again, as charity or pity, hiding itself beneath almost infinite disguises, the sight of which causes my heart almost to faint within me.

"Behold also what blindness self-love occasions between God and man, and know that no evil can be so great as this; yet man does not perceive it, but seems to hold it as salutary, and to rejoice over what ought rather to make him weep.

"There is no doubt that, if man could perceive the many difficulties thrown by self-love in the way of his own good, he would no longer allow himself to be deceived by it; and its malignity is the more to be dreaded because it is so powerful that were but one grain of it in the world would be sufficient to corrupt all mankind. Wherefore I conclude that self-love is the root of all evils which exist in this world and in the other. Behold Lucifer, whose present state is the result of following the suggestions of his self-love; and in ourselves it seems to me even worse. Our father Adam has so contaminated us that to my eyes the evil appears almost incurable, for it so penetrates our veins, our nerves, our bones, that we can neither say nor think nor do anything which is not full of the poison of this love—not even those thoughts and deeds which are directed toward the purification of the spirit.

"For so great and hopeless an infirmity no remedy can be found but God, and if he does not heal us in this world by his grace, our defects must needs be cleansed hereafter by the fire of purgatory; it being necessary, before it is possible for us to behold the pure face of God, that we should be freed from all our stains. And, therefore, when I see how rigorous and severe is this purgation, and that it is not in man's power to escape from self-love, or to see and understand the dangers of its hidden venom as it is necessary that he should, I long to cry out in a voice that should even pierce the heavens, 'God help me, God help me,' and continue this cry so long as life remains to me.

"Consider, then, that if this love is of such force that it makes man regardless of life or death, heaven or hell, how incomparably greater must that divine love be, which God himself infuses by his great goodness into our hearts. This love, unlike the other, has an eye not only to the welfare of our souls and bodies, but to those of our neighbor, and is careful to preserve his honor and his goods. It is benignant and gentle in all things and to all men; it renounces its self-will, and accepts instead the will of God, to whom it always submits. God, moreover, by his incomparable love, so inflames, purifies, illuminates, and fortifies its will that it no longer fears anything but sin, because that alone displeases God; and, therefore, rather than commit the least sin, it would choose to undergo the most atrocious torments that can be imagined.

"This is one of the effects of the divine love which gives man such liberty, peace, and contentment that he seems almost to enjoy heaven while yet in this life, and is so absorbed that he can neither speak, nor think, nor desire aught beside.

"This divine love, which thus separates us from the world and from ourselves in order to unite us to God, is our only true and proper love. When, then, it has been thus infused into our hearts, what more can we desire in this world or in the other? Death becomes a thing longed after, and hell loses its terrors for the soul which loves; for it dreads nothing but sin, which alone can separate it from its beloved. Oh, if men, and especially those who love, could only know how great and heavy a thing it is to offend God, they would know it to be the greatest hell that could be suffered: he who has once enjoyed this sweet and gentle love, and lost it through any fault of his, would suffer agonies like those of the condemned souls, and esteem no toils too great by which he might once more regain it. Long experience has taught me that the love of God is our life, our bliss, and our repose, and that self-love is continual weariness, misery, and death both in this world and in the other."

CHAPTER XXIV

Concerning the three ways which God takes to purify the creature.

This holy Soul said: "I see three ways which God takes when he wishes to purify the creature.

"The first is when he gives it a love so stripped of all things that, even if it desired, it could neither see nor wish for anything but this love, which by reason of its poverty and simplicity, is able to detect every vestige of self-love; and, seeing the truth it can never be self-deceived, but is reduced to such despair of itself that it is unable to say or do anything which could afford it either corporal or spiritual consolation. And thus, by degrees, its self-love is destroyed, since it is certain that he who eats not, dies. Notwithstanding this, however, so great is the evil of self-love that it clings to man almost to the end of his life. I have seen this in myself, for, from time to time I have found many natural desires destroyed within me which had previously seemed to me very good and perfect; but when they were thus removed I saw that they had been depraved and faulty, and in accordance with those spiritual and bodily infirmities which, being hidden from me, I had not supposed myself to possess. And this is why it is necessary to attain such a subtlety of spiritual vision, in order that all which at first appears to us perfection may in the end be known as imperfections, robberies, and woes; all this is clearly revealed in that mirror of truth, pure love, in which all things appears distorted which to us had seemed upright.

"The second mode which I beheld, and which pleased me more than the first, is that in which God gives man a mind occupied with great suffering; for that makes him know himself, and how abject and vile he is. This vision of his own misery keeps him in great poverty, and deprives him of all things which could afford him any savor of good; thus his self-love is not able to nourish itself, and from lack of nourishment it wastes away until at last man understands that if God did not hold his hand, giving him his being, and removing from him this hateful vision, he could never issue from this hell. And when God is pleased to take away this vision of his utter hopelessness in himself, afterwards he remains in great peace and consolation.

"The third mode, which is still more excellent than either of these, is when God gives his creature a mind so occupied in him, that neither interiorly nor exteriorly is it able to think of anything but God, and those things which are his. Even the works which it performs it does not think of or hold in any esteem, except in so far as they are necessary to the love of God; and hence it seems like one dead to the world, for it is unable to delight itself in anything or to understand anything, even if it wished to do so, either in heaven or on earth; there is given to it also such a poverty of spirit that it knows neither what it has nor what it does, nor does it make any provision for what it should do, either with regard to God or to the world, for itself or for its neighbor, because it is not shown how it may do so, but is always held by God in union with him and in sweet confusion.

"In this way the soul remains rich, yet poor, unable to appropriate anything, or to nourish itself, because it is necessary that it should be lost and annihilated in itself, and thus find itself in God, in whom, in truth, it was from the beginning although it knew not how it was so.

"There is also the religious life, of which I will say nothing further, because all must pass through one of these three ways of which I have been speaking, and also because it has been sufficiently treated of by others."

CHAPTER XXV

The manner in which the saint was medically treated for bodily infirmity, when her suffering was from spiritual fire, and of other accidents that befell her.

The perfection of this saint, thus illuminated by God, the true light, could not be understood, for it did not manifest itself by outward acts but all her perfection was in the interior of her soul, in the view of herself and of her God, with whom she was united in an extraordinary manner, and also in secret interior conversations, some of which she repeated twice (although she could poorly utter them in words), not as they actually took place within, for they were unutterable, and she could only express them by similitudes.

The state of this soul was not passive, as it is wont to be with others, for so profound was her sense of the importance of what she saw, that it inflamed her heart to such a degree that she fell dangerously ill. It is easy to perceive from this, how far such a creature was removed from the common experience. Usually, men hardly feel any compunction for the sins they have committed, and of venial offences they scarcely make any account; but the body of the saint was almost rent in pieces when it was given her to see the greatness of even a venial sin, and if God had discovered to her one of these sins in herself, she certainly would have fallen dead.

Her sufferings were often so great that recourse was had to medical treatment, and letting of blood was ordered to relieve the burning fire of the spirit and restore the power of speech, but with little effect. Medicines were also administered when she seemed near her end, but they increased her suffering, although she took them in obedience. It then began to be understood that

God was the author of these things, and she was left to struggle with her attacks without medicine, but it required great care and watchfulness to preserve her life. The devoted attendants who surrounded her were confounded, and she would sometimes say, in a voice scarcely audible: "Now my heart seems as if in ashes, I am consuming with love." At other times, to relieve her humanity, she would go into a solitary apartment, and there cast herself upon the ground, crying: "O love, I can bear no more;" and, writhing in agony, the house would resound with her cries and lamentations.

Sometimes, when walking in the garden, she would address the plants and trees, saying: "Are you not creatures created by my God? are you not obedient to him?" And thus discoursing, she would obtain some relief to her sufferings, but if she perceived she was overheard, she suddenly stopped, and answered any one who spoke to her according to the necessities of the affairs of human life.

CHAPTER XXVI

Of the three things to which she could not consent, and of those which she could not refrain from desiring.

This soul had so close a union with God, and her free-will was brought into such subjection, that she felt no resistance nor choice, having conquered all things, more than humanity can comprehend; yet she said there were three things to two of which she could not consent, and a third which she could not but desire.

In the first place she could not consent to, nor commit any, even the smallest, sin. For having the greatest horror of sin, and having attained, through the sight of her own misery, to the greatest simplicity, she did not perceive it in others, and could not comprehend how men could consent to it, particularly to mortal sin; and if perchance she saw with her own eyes some inexcusable sin, still she could not understand that there could be in man the malice of sin, believing that others honored God as she honored him.

Secondly, and this, although obscure to the imperfect intellect, was clear to her, she could not unite with the will of God in suffering so cruel a passion, and she would rather have endured all the pains of all the souls in hell, than that her Love should suffer such punishment.

The third thing, and it was this that she could not refrain from desiring, was holy communion; for the holy communion is nothing but God himself. And in this she testified the great reverence and honor in which she held priests, namely, by affirming that if the priest had not been willing to give her communion, she would have taken it patiently, and not persisted;

but wishing to receive communion, she could not say that she did not wish it.

CHAPTER XXVII

Of the sweetness of the divine precepts, and the advantage of temporal adversity.

All things took place in this holy soul in the order of true love; and she sometimes said to her Lord: "O Love! If others are bound to keep thy commandments, I am bound to keep them by a tenfold obligation, because they are sweet and full of love. Thou dost not command things that lead to evil; but to him who obeys thou givest great peace, love, and union with thyself. This cannot be understood by one who has not experienced it; for the divine precepts, although they are contrary to sensuality, are yet in accordance with the spirit which, by its nature, seeks separation from all the bodily senses, by union with God, to which union I find every other love of things inferior to God to be a hindrance."

She saw that all things are necessary which God ordains, who is only waiting to consume interiorly and exteriorly all our corrupt affections, and that all wrongs, injuries, contempt, sickness, poverty, abandonment of relatives and friends, the temptations of the devil, mortifications, and all else contrary to humanity, are especially needful to us, that we may combat with them, till at length gaining through them the victory, our corrupt affections may be extinguished, until adversity appears to us no longer bitter, but sweet.

Whoever believes that anything good or bad can befall him, which can separate him from God, shows that he is not yet strong in divine charity; for man should fear nothing but to offend God, and all beside should be to him as if it were not. For herself, she said, that she seemed to see in her heart a ray of love proceeding from God, binding them together with a golden thread, and had no fear that it would ever be loosed; and this had been the case ever since her conversion. Her sweet Lord gave her such confidence that when she was moved to pray for anything, something within seemed to say: "Command, for love can do it." Indeed she had every thing she asked, with all possible certainty.

She was wont to say: "The love of God is our proper love, for we are created for that alone; the love, on the contrary, for everything beside, ought in truth to be termed hatred, since it deprives us of our proper love, which is God. Love then God, who loves thee, and leave him who does not love thee, namely, everything beneath God; for all things are enemies to that true love. Oh! that I could make this truth be felt as I myself feel it: I am certain that there is no creature who would not love Him; so that if the sea were the food of love, there are no men or women, who would not drown themselves in it, and those who were at a distance from it would always be drawing nearer to it, that they might plunge into it; for every pleasure, when compared to it, is pain, and such riches does it confer on a man, that all beside should seem to him but misery.

"It makes him so light that he does not feel the earth beneath his feet; his affections are so fixed on things above that he loses all sense of suffering here below, and he is so free, that there is nothing to keep him from the presence of God. If you asked me: 'What dost thou feel?' I should answer thee: 'What eye could not see, nor ear hear;' but I am ashamed to speak of it in my poor language, for I am certain that all I can say of God, is not of God, but only fragments that fall from his table."

CHAPTER XXVIII

The process of annihilation of man in God illustrated by the figure of the eating of bread.—Of her interior and exterior.

"Take a loaf," said the saint, "and eat it, and after you have eaten it, its substance goes to the nutriment of the body, and what is superfluous passes away; for if nature retained it, having no need of it, the body would die. Now if that bread should say to the body: Why do you deprive me of my existence, for by my nature I am not satisfied to be thus reduced to nothingness? If I could, I would defend myself from thee, for it is natural for every creature to preserve itself,—the body would answer: Bread, thy being is designed for my support, which is more worthy than thee, and hence thou shouldst be more content with the end for which thou wast created, than with thy own being; for if it were not for thy end, thy being would have no value but to be thrown aside, as something worthless and dead. It is thy end which gives thee a dignity to which thou canst not attain but by means of thy annihilation. If thou wouldst live for thy end, thou wouldst care for thy being, but wouldst say: Quickly, quickly, take me from myself, and let me attain my end for which I am created."

This soul became so detached, both exteriorly and interiorly, that she could no longer perform her accustomed exercises, for she had lost all vigor of mind and body. She had no desire to confess; but going to confession, as usual, she found that she had no part in any sin; and when she attempted to mention her offences generally, it seemed to her that she was deceiving; and through her entire detachment she was in possession of the greatest peace, of which she was never divested.

CHAPTER XXIX

The saint urged to give an idea of her state.

Of free-will this blessed one said, that when she considered carefully her vocation, she saw such great things effected by God in her, that it almost seemed as if she had been forced by him, for she could nowhere see her own consent, but rather it seemed to her that she had resisted, especially in the beginning, and the sense of this had inflamed her with a burning love. But generally, when speaking of it, she said: "God first arouses man from sin, then with the light of faith illuminates the intellect, and afterwards, with a certain satisfaction and zeal, inflames the will. And Almighty God does this in an instant, although we tell it in many words, and measure it by time."

When the saint was sometimes urged by her spiritual children to give them an idea of her state in words, she would tell them it was impossible, but on one occasion she allowed a religious to interpret it, in order to gratify his desire to understand it better, which he did to her great satisfaction and joy; wherefore, with a benignant countenance, she exclaimed: "Oh my dear child, it is as you have said, and hearing you I feel that it is thus. You have said all that can be said, but the effect is incomprehensible." Then the religious said to her: "Oh mother, cannot you ask of God, your Love, some little drops of it for your children?" and she answered joyfully: "I see this sweet Love so gracious to his children, that I can ask nothing for them, but that I may present them in his presence."

This creature became at length like a cherub to look upon, so that she gave great consolation to every one who beheld her; and those who visited her found it hard to leave her. When she was about sixty-three years of age, her heart was inflamed anew with a ray of love. This dart was so powerful and penetrating, that she felt as if severely wounded in the region of the heart, and she suffered great bodily pain. After some days she was again inflamed with love, and it always seemed to her that the last wound was the greatest.

CHAPTER XXX

Of her compunction for having desired death, every desire being an imperfection.—She relates her conversion to one of her spiritual children.

In the year 1507, while present at the office for the dead, she felt a desire to die. It was a desire of the soul that it might quit the body and be united with God. The body also desired it, that it might be freed from the torment which it suffered from the flames of love in the soul; these however, were only natural desires, to which her will gave no consent.

And as her desire was inspired by her Love who wished to purify her, and not from her will, as soon as she felt it, she suddenly exclaimed: "O Love, I desire nothing but thee, and in thy own way: but if it please thee, who dost not wish that I should die, neither that I should desire death, let me at least be present at the death and burial of others, that I may see in them that blessedness that is not bestowed on me." Love consented to this, and for some time she was present at the death and burial of all those who died in the hospital, without any desire to die herself. And by degrees, the union of love increasing in that purified heart, she lost the desire to see others die, but still, whenever she spoke of death, she seemed filled with a new and joyful emotion.

At one time when she fell into ecstasies, and appeared as if dead, the persons around her, who did not understand her state, believed her to be suffering from what is commonly called vertigo. She herself, through humility and a desire to be unnoticed, on speaking of it to a religious, also called it vertigo: but the religious answered: "Mother, you need not use concealment with me: I entreat you for the honor and glory of

God, to choose some person who will be satisfactory to you, and narrate to him the graces with which God has favored you, that when you are gone these graces may not remain hidden and unknown, and the praise and glory of God arising from them be lost." To which she answered: "It shall be as you wish, if it is the will of my sweet Love;" and she would choose no other than himself who had given her this counsel, although she knew it would be impossible for her to narrate the smallest part of those interior communications between God and the soul; and of the exterior, she had experienced almost nothing.

At another time, in conversation with the same religious, she began to narrate her conversion and many other things, as well as she could, which have been faithfully collected and introduced into the present volume.

CHAPTER XXXI

How the saint left the whole care of herself to Love; and what means Love employed to purify her from her imperfections.

When Love had taken upon himself the care and control of everything, he never more abandoned it. "And I," said the saint, "gave the keys of the house to Love, with full power to do all that was necessary, and I took no heed of body or soul, friends, relatives, or the world; but of all that the law of pure love requires I took care that the least part should not be wanting. And when I saw Love accepting the charge, and producing the effect, I turned towards him, and was occupied in watching this, his work. And he made me look upon many things as unjust and imperfect, which before had appeared to myself and others as just and perfect, and in everything was found defects. If I spoke of spiritual things, Love suddenly checked me, telling me that I must not speak, but let the flame burn on within, no word and no act escaping which should serve to refresh either soul or body.

"One day I asked my confessor if I should try to eat, that I might not cause any injury to the soul or body. Love answered me within, and my confessor from without: 'Who is this who speaks of eating or not eating, under the form of a motive? Be silent, for I know you, and you cannot deceive me.' Finding his eye so acute and powerful, I gave up all to him, asking God to do with me what seemed to him good; to strip me of all things and clothe me with his simple, pure, powerful, great, and burning love.

"And then Love exclaimed: 'It is my will to leave every one naked, naked; neither will I have anything above me nor under me. And be it known to you, that such is my nature and condition, that I convert and change into myself all souls that can be changed, despoiling them of self.' Love will be alone. If another should be in his company, the gates of heaven would be closed against him, for they are open only to pure Love. Let each one, then, leave himself to be guided by Love, that he may be conducted to that end which pure Love desires all to attain.

"Pure Love draws the soul to himself in a variety of ways, and when he sees her occupied with any affection, he marks all things that she loves as his enemies, and consumes them without sparing herself or her body; and although the nature of Love would destroy them by one blow, yet seeing the weakness of man, he cuts away little by little, and silently; for we cling so firmly to the object of our love, which we esteem beautiful, good, and just, that we will listen to nothing that opposes us; therefore Love says: 'I will put my hand to the work, for with words I can do nothing; I will destroy all things that thou lovest, by death, infirmity, or poverty; by hatred and discord; by detraction, scandal, lies, and infamy; by relatives, by friends, and by thyself, till thou knowest not what to do, finding thyself cast out from all things that constituted thy delight, and receiving from them only pain and confusion; neither dost thou understand these operations of divine Love, all of which seem contrary to reason, both as regards God and the world; therefore thou dost cry and lament, striving and hoping to escape from this distress, and thou wilt never escape from it.'

"When divine Love has kept a soul thus in suspense, and, as it were, desperate, and disgusted with all things that before she loved, then he shows her himself with his divinely joyful and radiant countenance, and as soon as the soul perceives it, naked and destitute she casts herself into his hands, crying: 'O blind one, what didst thou seek? what hast thou desired! here are all the delights thou hast sought! O divine Love, how sweetly hast thou deceived me in order to strip me of all self-love and clothe me with pure love abounding with every delight! Now that I see the truth, I have nothing to lament but my ignorance.'"

CHAPTER XXXII

How well regulated was the saint in all things.—Of the opposition of her spirit to humanity, and how humanity tormented her.

With this blessed soul everything was so well ordered, that wherever she had control, or could offer a remedy, she never could endure any disorder; and she could neither live nor converse with persons who were not well regulated, especially if they were those who appeared to have entered with herself the way of perfection; and when she saw them countenancing any imperfection, and taking part in any of those things which she had learned to abhor, she left their company.

She was very compassionate to all creatures, although merciless to their defects, so that when an animal was killed, or a tree cut down, she could hardly bear to see them lose the life that God had given them, but she would have been very severe in rooting out the evil from one who had brought it upon himself by sin.

She could not see her own sins, or realize that she must sometimes commit them, neither could she believe that others would sin; and so entire was the peace of her mind, that it seemed to substitute for bodily sleep. Such repose was, however, more refreshing to her body than natural sleep, for sleep takes off the mind from God. She was so restrained interiorly, that she was wont to say: "If I uttered a word, breathed a sigh, or cast a glance towards any person who could understand me, my humanity would be well content, as a thirsty person when given a drink." Meaning by this that when she was pierced by the arrows of divine love, she lost all feeling and remained motionless, until God, as it often happened, relieved her from this occupation.

So opposite and repugnant was the spirit to humanity, that when humanity wept, the spirit laughed, and held her in such subjection as to reprove her, not only for every unnecessary action, but for every word, not permitting those around to offer her any alleviation in her trials, seeming ever lovingly to mock her by exciting her desires for these things with which she was accustomed to console herself, allowing her to taste all things, and then suddenly destroying all relish for them, till by degrees she had none left for any earthly thing, and could find no exterior or interior nourishment, and in this desolation a secret longing would come over her to hide herself, and weep, and lament.

Sometimes she would cast herself into the hedge of rose trees in the garden, and seize the thorns with both hands, without feeling the pain, so entire was the occupation of her mind. She would bite and burn her hands, to relieve the interior suffering that consumed her, and the most extreme external pain she esteemed as nothing. Her body was often so deserted by the spirit, that without any resistance on her part four persons could not move her from her seat. All these things were not done voluntarily, but by a spontaneous impulse; neither did she find any consolation upon the earth, but was constrained to shun those things without which others cannot live.

She found no solace except in her confessor, with whom she had an interior and exterior correspondence. But he, too, was taken from her, and her sufferings greatly increased, because there was nothing to which she could have recourse either in Heaven or on earth, and she was wont to say: "I am in this world like one who is away from home, who has left all his relatives and friends, and finds himself in a foreign land; when having accomplished the business for which he was sent he is ready to leave and go home, where his heart and mind are; for so ardent is his love of his own country, that a day of absence seems a year."

She felt herself every day more and more restrained, like one who is confined at first within the walls of a city; then in a house without a garden, now in a hall, now in a chamber, then again in an antechamber; sometimes in a dimly lighted, remote apartment, then in a dark prison, her hands tied, her feet chained, her eyes bandaged, and without food; for no one could speak with her and she was left without hope of release but by death; she had no consolation but the knowledge that it is a merciful God who does all this in his love; and with this she was satisfied.

On one occasion, hearing some one repeat the words: "Arise, arise, ye dead, and come to judgment;" she cried aloud, in the excess of love: "Would that I could come now, now;" and all who heard her were astonished. With that burning love in her heart, it seemed to her that she could pass through the most searching judgment; for she saw nothing in herself for that judgment to condemn; she even took pleasure in the thought of it, for she earnestly desired to see the infinitely powerful and just judge, who makes all things tremble, except pure and simple love.

CHAPTER XXXIII

How an evil spirit, that had possession of one of her spiritual daughters, named her Catherine Serafina.

This holy soul had, in the house with her, a spiritual daughter who was tormented by the devil, who frequently attacked her, even throwing her upon the ground, and by this violence driving her almost to desperation. This evil spirit even entered into her mind, and prevented her from thinking of divine things, so that it seemed to her that she was separated from God, and lost. She was beside herself, and fell so entirely under his diabolical will, that she became almost a demon herself. She was insupportable to herself, and found no peace except in the presence of her spiritual mother; for when they were together, at a glance they understood each other, one having the spirit of God, and the other its opposite.

One day this afflicted creature, vexed by the unclean spirit, knelt at the feet of the blessed Catherine, in the presence of their confessor; and the devil through her said: "We are both slaves by reason of that pure love that thou hast in thy heart." and then, enraged with himself for having uttered these words, cast her upon the ground, winding about like a serpent. When she had risen from the ground, the confessor said: "What is the name of this woman, tell me," and the evil spirit answered: Catherine, and would say no more. Then the confessor said: "Tell me her surname, is it Adorno or Fieschi?" and he would not answer; but the confessor insisted, and he at length said: Catherine Serafina, but he uttered these words struggling with great agony.

This afflicted being possessed a powerful intellect, and she lived in virginity. The Lord, perhaps, sent this affliction upon her to keep her humble. She died a holy death, but the evil spirit never left her until the very last moment.

CHAPTER XXXIV

How the Saint gained a spiritual director.[1]

The blessed Catherine, while reflecting on the opposition between pure love and the evil spirit, was accustomed to say that man did not consider the difference, and did not appreciate extreme love as he ought, "For truly," she added, "he who does not know precious stones, does not value them."

And, filled with compassion for the blindness of man, she said: "If by taking my blood and giving it to man to drink, I could make known to him this truth, I would give it all for love of him. I cannot endure the thought that man, created for the good that I see and know, should lose it

Catherine persevered in this way for about twenty-five years, instructed and directed by God alone, by a wonderful, divine operation. Afterwards, perhaps on account of the approach of old age and her extreme weakness, the Lord sent a director who took charge of her soul and of her bodily health; a spiritual person of holy life, in every way fitted for such a charge, to whom God gave the light and grace to know his designs in regard to her. He was chosen rector of the hospital where she lived, he heard her confessions, said mass for her, and gave her communion, whenever he could do so.

This priest, at the request of some spiritual persons who were devoted to the saint, wrote most of the present work, having urged and induced her to relate the extraordinary graces which God had conferred upon her, especially as this religious, by long

---

[1] The division of chapters 33 and 34 was missing from the source material and has been added by the present editor.

intercourse, well understood the order of her life. The first time that she made her confession to him, she said: "Father, I know not where I am, as to my soul or my body. I wish to confess, but I do not see any offence that I have committed." And the faults that she enumerated did not seem to her sins of thought, word, or deed; for she was like a child who, when in his childishness he ignorantly does something which he is told is wrong, suddenly changes color, and blushes, but not because he is sensible to the fault.

She sometimes said to her confessor: "I do not know how to make my confession, for I have not enough exterior or interior feeling to be able to accuse myself of having said those things on account of which I feel some stings of conscience. I would not fail to make my confession, and I do not know whom I am to accuse of my sins; I would accuse myself, but I cannot."

When God was effecting anything within her that troubled her, she submitted it entirely to her confessor, and conferred with him; and he, by the divine light and grace, understood the whole, giving her such replies that he seemed to feel what she felt. This was a great consolation to her, so that she spoke to him with entire confidence, and could not be satisfied until she had discovered to him all she felt. When she was prevented from communicating to him anything that was upon her mind, she felt as if in burning flames, but after she had spoken of it to her father, she was tranquil and satisfied.

It was a great consolation to her that he could understand her by a glance, when she could not speak, allaying the violence of the burning fire within, and strengthening her exhausted frame. The interior action was so intense that it became necessary to divert her mind by external things, and that diversion was torture to her, for it did violence to her heart. At one time, having been in a weak state for several days, she took the hand of her confessor and raised it to her face, and the odor of it penetrated her heart with such a fullness of exterior and interior sweetness that it seemed supernatural.

The confessor asking her what was the nature of that odor, she answered that it was an odor that God had sent to comfort the soul and body in their sufferings; that it was so penetrating and sweet that it seemed as if it could bring the dead to life, and she added: "Since God grants it to me, I shall console myself with it so long as it pleases him." The confessor, believing that as it was given through him he too could perceive it, raised his own hand to smell the fragrance of it, but there was none there, and it was told him that God does not give his good things to those who seek them, but only bestows them in cases of necessity, and for some great spiritual result.

The saint also said that she was permitted to see that this odor was a drop of the beatitude that the body with its senses will enjoy in heaven, through the humanity of our Lord Jesus Christ; by which every one will be satisfied eternally in body as well as soul. Her body and soul were strengthened and refreshed for several days by the impression and remembrance of this odor.

On one occasion she said to her confessor, who was sometimes absent from her: "It seems to me that God has given you the care of me alone, and that you ought not to attend to any one else; for I have persevered during the twenty-five years in the spiritual life without the help of any creature, but now that I cannot endure such interior and exterior conflicts, God has sent you to me. If you know how terribly I suffer when you are absent, you would rather remain with me in my trials, than go in search of any recreation; and yet I would not ask you not to go."

And indeed it appeared as if every remedy and relief that God allowed to her soul and body was given her by this confessor, who, at the moment provided her with thoughts and words, which were suited to her necessities, so that he was amazed at them himself, and when the occasion for them was past, no remembrance of them remained.

And because this continual intercourse and close familiarity roused some to murmur who did not understand the necessity for them, the confessor withdrew and was absent for three days, to ascertain whether this necessity was wholly divine without any human mixture, and to relieve himself from every scruple; but he repented making the trial, on account of the severe sufferings of the saint. Moreover, he was in secret reproved by God for his incredulity, when he had been so long a witness to so many supernatural signs, one of which would have been sufficient to convert a Jew; and after this his scruples never returned.

The saint continued for many years in this state of dependence on her confessor, and by the grace of God, through all his attendance upon her, in his fatigues and trials, his health never failed. When she concealed from him any interior operation, it was intimated to him by some divine inspiration, and he would say to her: "You have such and such a thing on your mind, and you wish to deny it to me, but God will not permit you." At these words she was greatly surprised, and acknowledged that they were true, and afterwards was freed from her sufferings. Sometimes she would say to her confessor: "What do you think is in my mind?" and although he knew nothing of it, yet at that moment words were given him, and he told her the whole.

CHAPTER XXXV

Treatment of the saint by her husband, and how she obtained salvation of his soul from God, and also that of Sister Tommasa Fiesca, her companion.

As we have mentioned before, this creature, so favored by God, was married at the age of sixteen to Giuliano Adorno, who, although of a noble family, was of a perverse and stubborn temper, and conducted his affairs so badly, that he was reduced to poverty; yet she was always obedient, and patient with his whims and eccentricities, but at the same time she suffered so much from him that with difficulty she preserved her health, and became to reduced and wasted, that she was a most pitiable object. She lived in a solitary house, alone, to satisfy him, and never went out except to attend mass, and then return as quickly as possible, for she would endure anything rather than give pain to others.

Almighty God, seeing that this soul could be brought to great perfection, enabled her to support all this, without murmuring, in silence, and with the greatest patience. For the first few years she was kept in such subjection that she knew nothing of what was going on in the world; but, during the five following she sought to divert herself from the great vexations which her husband caused her, by associating with other ladies, and occupying herself with the affairs of the world as they did.

But she was soon after called by the Lord, and left this way of life, never to return to it again; and, by the goodness of God, she was permitted to live with her husband, as a sister with a brother. Her husband became a member of the third order of St. Francis, and finally was visited by a severe illness, which he bore so impatiently that his wife became greatly distressed for the salvation of his soul. As his end approached, she withdrew into a retired apartment, and there, with tears and sobs, implored her sweet Love to save him, saying, "O Love, I beg of thee this soul: I pray thee give it to me, for thou canst do it." Persevering in this for the space of half an hour, an interior voice at length assured her that she was heard, and returning to her husband's chamber, she found him so calm and changed, that, by every word and act, he manifested his submission to the divine will.

This miracle was made known by the blessed one herself to a spiritual child of hers after the death of her husband. "My son," said she, "Giuliano is gone: you know his eccentricity, which caused me so much suffering during his life, but before he passed away, my sweet Love assured me of his salvation." It was plain that God had caused her to say this, that the miracle might be made known; for, afterwards, Catherine seemed to regret that she had spoken on the subject, but the person being very prudent, made no remark and began to talk of other things. After her husband had passed away in holy peace, and was buried, her friends would say to her that she was relieved from great trials, and to human reason she indeed appeared to be released from great oppression, but she answered that she was not conscious of it, that all things were the same to her, and that she only cared to do the will of God.

She also lost some of her brothers and sisters but so closely was she united with the sweet will of God, that she did not suffer any more than if they had not been her own kindred. And on account of this she could not understand why one of her companions of the same house of Fieschi as herself, and married as she was, should leave the world by degrees, for fear of turning back. After the death of her husband, this person became a nun in a convent of the Observantines of St. Dominic, called also St. Silvester; and twenty years after her profession, she was transferred to another convent of the same order, called the New Monastery, that she might reform it by introducing a stricter observance. She was called Sister Tommasa, was full of prudence and sanctity, and attained great perfection. She was superior of that monastery, and so burning was her zeal, that she was accustomed to write, compose, paint, and practice various devout exercises, in order to mitigate its violence. She wrote a treatise on the Apocalypse, and upon Dionysius the Areopagite, and other beautiful, devout, and edifying pieces. She painted with her own hand many holy countenances; the most remarkable is one of Piety, representing a certain very holy mystery, when the priest is consecrating at the altar. She wrought very delicately with her needle many pious subjects, among which is still seen in her first monastery, God the Father, surrounded by angels, with Christ and other figures of saints worked with great skill and dignity.

Many things are told of this mother's devout life and exemplary conversation, so full of the fervor of divine love, by the nuns of her first and second convents, as well as by pious seculars who were her friends; also how happily she passed from this life praising the Lord. Her death took place in the year 1534, when she was more than 86 years of age. As we have mentioned, the blessed Catherine wondered how (when she was yet in the world) she could make such slow progress in contempt of the world; but she herself, on the other hand, said that Catherine, for so she called her, considered her desperate; and that it would be a dreadful mortification to her if she should turn back; Catherine was more surprised at this thought of turning back, and could not understand it. "If I should turn back," she said, "I should not only wish my eyes to be put out, but that every kind of punishment and insult should be inflicted on me."

The wonderful designs of God are manifested in these two women, belonging to the same period, and both married; one of whom was converted by infused grace and at once made perfect, while the other arrived at perfection by virtue slowly acquired.

CHAPTER XXXVI

How a person, hopelessly ill, was cured by the prayers of the saint.

A man named Marco dal Sale, who was suffering from a cancer of his nose, after trying every remedy that could be devised by the skill of physicians, and finding no relief, became almost desperately impatient. His wife Argentina, seeing his condition, went to the hospital where the holy Catherine lived, and begged her to visit her sick husband, and pray the Lord for him; and the saint, as if under obedience, complied.

This blessed soul was so obedient, that if an ant had come to ask her to perform some act of mercy, she would at once have followed it. Catherine, having arrived at the house of the sick man, somewhat consoled him by a few humble and devout words. Returning afterwards to the hospital with Argentina, they entered a church called St. Mary of Grace, and there kneeling, Catherine was moved to pray for the sick man. Having finished her prayer, she returned with Argentina to the hospital, and when the latter had taken eave of her and gone home, she found her husband so changed, that from a demon he had almost become an angel, and, turning to Argentina, he exclaimed with joy and tenderness; "Oh! Argentina, tell me who is that holy soul whom you have brought here?" and Argentina answered: "It is Madonna Catherine Adorno, whose life is most perfect." The sick man then implored her, by the love of God, that she would bring her there again. The next day she complied with is request, and having related to St. Catherine what occurred, brought her home with her again.

She knew, however, beforehand, the condition of this sick man, in the answer to her secret prayer; for she never made a special prayer except when interiorly moved to it by her Love, by which also she knew that it was favorably heard. When she entered the room the sick man saluted her, and continued weeping for some time, then said: "The reasons why I have asked you to come here again are, first, to thank you for your charity towards me, and then to ask of you one more favor, which I pray you not to deny me. After you left me, our Lord Jesus Christ himself appeared visibly to me, under the form in which he appeared to Magdalene in the garden, gave me his most holy blessing, pardoned my sins, and said that he appeared to me, because on Ascension Day I was to go to him; therefore, I pray you, most kind mother, that you may be pleased to accept Argentina as your spiritual daughter, retaining her always near you; and I pray you, Argentina, to consent to this." Both answered him joyfully that they were content. After Catherine had gone, the sick man sent for an Augustinian Father from a monastery called the Consolation, and having carefully made his confession and received communion, summoned a notary and his relatives, and arranged all his affairs, satisfying every one. They all thought that his sufferings had turned his head, and told him to be comforted, that he would soon recover and that there was no need of his attending to these things; but he was too wise to be influenced by their persuasions. The vigil of the Ascension having arrived, he sent again for his confessor, again made his confession, and received holy communion; then he received extreme unction with recommendation of the soul, all with great devotion, in preparation for his journey. Night coming on, he said to his confessor: "Return to your monastery, and when the time comes, I will send for you. Every one having gone, he was left alone with his wife, and turning towards her with the crucifix in his hand, said: "Argentina! I leave you this for your spouse, prepare to suffer, for I assure you that you will have to do so," which she indeed did, both mentally and from long continued bodily infirmity. He passed the night in exhorting and encouraging her to give herself entirely to God, to be willing to endure suffering, which is the ladder of ascent to heaven. When it was day, he said: "Argentina, God be with you, for the hour is come," and having uttered these words, he expired, and his spirit knocked at the window of his confessor's cell, crying: Ecce Homo; which when the confessor heard, he knew that Marco had passed to his Lord.

After the burial of Marco, the blessed Catherine received Argentina as her spiritual daughter, according to her promise, and this by a divine dispensation, for, if she had not had such a spiritual child, she could not have lived in the state of abstraction in which she was often thrown by the burning fires of her sweet Love. As she loved this daughter of hers very much, she took her with her whenever she went out; and one day when they were passing the before-mentioned church, Our Lady of Grace, she entered, and after making her devotions, she said to Argentina: "This is the place where grace was obtained for your husband." The Lord permitted her to say this, that the miracle might be made known for our edification.

Chapter XXXVII

Continuing an account of her extraordinary way of life, and her wonderful condition for some time before her death.

For nearly nine years before her death, the saint suffered from a malady not understood by physicians or by any one else. It was not a bodily infirmity; neither did it seem to her a spiritual operation; and it was very difficult on the part of those who attended her to know how to treat it. Medicine was of no avail, still less the support obtained from bodily sustenance; but at length a way was found to control it.

She was greatly debilitated, so that at times she appeared to be near her end. For a year before her death she did not eat in a week what another would require for one meal, and for the last six months she only took a little broth, refusing everything else.

She never omitted holy communion, except when absolutely unable to receive it, and in that case she suffered more from the deprivation than from all her infirmities: indeed, it seemed as if she could not live without this most holy sacrament. The vehemence of her spirit became at length so great that it shattered her bodily frame from head to foot; so that there was not a limb or nerve that was not tormented by her inward fires. She threw off blood and other substances, so that it was thought that she retained nothing even of the very little she ate; and for the last two weeks she took nothing but the most holy communion. She could not sleep, her suffering was so intense, and her screams were dreadful.

The burning interior and exterior flames prevented her from moving or being moved. Her sufferings banished from her all friends and spiritual persons who could offer her any relief, so that she remained in perfect interior and exterior solitude. And she suffered, too, in another way. Her humanity would sometimes crave food so extremely, that it would make any effort to obtain it; and when it was offered, the appetite was gone and she could not taste it, but remained patient in her hunger.

She was so entirely abandoned to her sufferings, that she appeared as if transfixed to the cross, with no desire but for the blessed sacrament. On the other hand, she was so happy, and uttered such burning words of divine love, that all around her wept from emotion. Many persons came from a distance to see her, and speak with her, and recommended themselves to her, believing that they had been a creature more divine than human, as in truth she was. They beheld heaven in her soul, and purgatory in her agonized body.

She saw the condition of the souls in purgatory in the mirror of her humanity and of her mind, and therefore spoke of it so clearly. She seemed to stand on a wall separating this life from the other, that she might relate in one what she saw suffered in the other.

We are told of St. Ignatius, that after his martyrdom his heart was opened, and on it was found inscribed, in letters of gold, the sweet name of Jesus, and who can doubt that if the heart of this loving servant of God had been opened, some wonderful mark would have been found upon it. The burning flames within even changed the color of the flesh about her heart, and if fire was applied to her body, she did not feel it, so much more powerful was the interior flame. But there is this difference between material fire and the flames of divine love, that the one consumes and destroys, while the other sustains and strengthens.

Chapter XXXVIII

How the sufferings she was to endure were revealed to her in spirit; and how dreadful they were to her humanity.—Seeing an image of the woman of Samaria, she asked of God that water.— Of a difference that arose between the spirit and humanity, and of other wonderful things.

Many graces were bestowed on this soul chosen of God, and many divine works were accomplished in her, during the year before she passed from this life to the Lord. And as things which take place suddenly cause greater terror, God revealed to her, at a glance, the order of his operations, and that she must die in great suffering, and made manifest to her this suffering, even her death. When humanity heard this she became almost frantic, and it seemed as if the soul must leave the body, for she could not utter a word.

When this terrible picture was removed, this holy soul uttered words of such ardent and inflamed love, that all present trembled at them; and although they were not understood by them, yet they were filled with wonder at beholding such an effect. While the revelation was taking place, the soul remained as lifeless as the body, having no sensibility to anything spiritual, being like one dead. She could not speak of this spiritual sight, neither give any idea of it, but her gestures and motions appeared so wonderful as to strike with awe and astonishment every beholder.

Her confessor was filled with dread at these things, considering the strict account to be rendered to God at the hour of death, when nothing is excused. What he beheld, remained impressed on his mind, and preyed upon it for many days.

When the spirit was occupied intently with divine Love, and heeded not whether humanity lived or died, so long as the soul could remain with God, humanity expostulated, saying: "You cannot continue in this way, and live. God does not design that I should yet die; and, certainly, you would do nothing but by the divine will. As I must live, whether you will or not, you must quit this burning flame, and condescend to bear with me, so long as it may please God; although I am sure that at any rate you will make me suffer enough; for every day you are gaining power, and becoming more intent on accomplishing your purpose, and in the end you will surely conquer."

When the spirit found itself obliged to yield somewhat to humanity, if it had not been restrained by a divine power, it would have reduced that body to dust, to obtain the liberty to be entirely occupied with itself; and the body, on its side, would rather have endured a thousand deaths than suffer so much from the oppression of the spirit; and in its distress it would often exclaim: "Oh, wretched that I am! to be engaged in so frightful a conflict;" then, addressing the spirit it would say: "I know that you cannot endure me, because I hold you bound on earth, in exile, and deprived of the fruition of the unbounded love of God; but I cannot sustain this fire of the love of God, rather would I endure any other torture than one day in its burning flames."

The spirit gradually consumed the human part, and reduced it to such exterior and interior weakness that it could no longer complain or make any of its former demonstrations. And the blessed one could sometimes only utter such words as these: Love of God, Sweetness of God, Purity of God. At another time she would be continually repeating: Charity, union, and peace; and sometimes only one word: God, God. At last she said nothing, for all her powers were confined within. On one occasion her heart was kindled by so burning a flame of love, that she could not endure it, and turning to a picture of the Samaritan woman at the well, she cried out: "O Lord, I pray thee, give me a drop of that water which thou givest to the Samaritan," and instantly a drop of that divine water was given to her, which refreshed her more than human tongue can describe.

Sometimes the conflict between humanity and the spirit was so great that the soul found herself, as it were, suspended in the air, drawn up by her intense desire to reach heaven, and yet attached to earth by her human and inferior part. At length the superior part so far conquered the inferior, that the latter became more and more detached from earth, and although at first this seemed strange to humanity, and she was discontented, yet she soon began to lose all attraction for earth, and to enjoy these things which the spiritual part enjoyed, till at length the attraction of the spirit so far prevailed, that the two became reconciled and were satisfied with the same food, although the human part did not entirely forget the earth; but she was ever receiving such tidings from heaven that she became constantly more firm, more persevering, more joyful and satisfied, so as by degrees to attain repose. This drawing of the spiritual part towards heaven was a means of purification, and the higher she ascended, the more she became detached from all things natural, awaiting the moment when she would leave the body at death, as the moment when she would leave purgatory for heaven; for God in his grace makes the body of some persons their purgatory.

This holy soul continually suffered more and more from the favors of divine love; sometimes for five or six days she could hardly breathe, so great was the vehemence of this inward fire; and every attack was more violent than the last, obliging her to conceal herself from all creatures, to avoid their observation and wonder at her extraordinary condition. Her body trembled like a leaf during these attacks, although her soul was in perfect peace; sometimes even blood would flow from her nose, and she was so reduced that, for several days, her strength would not return, and it was only restored to prepare her for a fresh attack.

CHAPTER XXXIX

How the spirit deprived her of her confessor, who concealed himself where he could witness her peace of mind in the midst of these tortures.—She had visions of angels.—Of the experiments tried by various physicians.—Of one who had come from England.—Of further divine operations.

On the 10th of January, 1510, during one of these attacks, all need of her confessor vanished from her mind, and she had no more desire to see him, either for the support and consolation of her body or her soul. She kept this thought secret for many hours, but expressed the contrary. This thought came from the spirit, who wished to deal with humanity without any intervention, and believed that the confessor, who thought she must do and say all she wished to do and say, might influence her too much, knowing, as she did, that all was by the ordinance of God.

When the confessor was removed, humanity was left desolate upon the earth, and could hardly endure herself, consuming away and yet living, because it was not God's time for her to die. The confessor at one time concealed himself to watch the operations of God in this soul. She locked herself into her chamber, alone; and, in her agony poured out her lamentations to her Lord, exclaiming: "O Lord! what dost thou wish me to do in this world? All my interior and exterior senses are lost. I find nothing in myself like other creatures, but I am like one dead; no creature understands me. I am alone, unknown, poor, naked, strange, and opposed to all the world; neither do I know what the world is, and therefore I can no longer dwell with creatures on the earth." She uttered these and many such expressions so piteously, that they would have melted the stones with compassion. The confessor, who was concealed and heard them all, was so moved that he was obliged to discover himself, and drawing near, spoke to her (for God had given him the grace), in such a manner that she remained consoled in body and mind for many days.

The sufferings of this blessed soul increased in violence, and her attacks became more frequent, and were sometimes too agonizing for human eyes to behold. She seemed writhing in flames of fire, and could not be kept upon her bed. Sometimes these tortures would continue for a day and night, without ceasing, and it seemed as if every moment must be her last. She lost sight and speech, but by signs asked that extreme unction might be given her, for she believed herself dying; but she lived to endure great sufferings, for through all that she had hitherto endured, she had remained in communication with God, and experienced great peace and interior joy in the midst of them; but now it was ordered that for a season she should be deprived of this divine communication, and should be left naked and desolate, with nothing to hold her to life but the conviction that this was the will of God concerning her. She would sometimes exclaim in her desolation: "It is now nearly thirty-five years, O my Lord, since I have asked anything of thee for myself; but now, most earnestly do I implore thee not to separate thyself from me. Thou well knowest, O Lord, that I could not endure it."

She said this because, from the time she was first called by God, her mind had always been in union with him, and at peace, and hence the separation appeared dreadful to her; her soul became more resigned, but humanity more tortured, at every fresh attack. When she was able to speak, her words appeared flames of divine love, and so penetrated the hearts of those who heard them, that they were deeply moved, and filled with astonishment.

On one occasion she had four excruciating attacks in one night. So great was the distress of her nerves, that from her head to her feet there was not a spot free from suffering; she cried aloud in her agony, and those around her implored God to have mercy on her, but she could find no relief, and yet she said, during a pause: "Tongue cannot tell, nor imagination conceive the peace of mind that I enjoy, but as to the human part, all the sufferings that man could inflict are nothing to the pains I endure; and in these operations the spirit and humanity are both watching to observe the doings of God. It is not the spirit, but humanity that cries out in agony."

In the intervals of this suffering, her body appeared in health, and free from any feverish affection. She laughed and spoke like a person in health, and told others that they must not be troubled on her account, for she was happy, but that they must strive to do right, for the ways of God were very strait.

She had at this time many visions of angels, and sometimes she was seen laughing with them. She smiled without speaking, and, as has been related, she beheld the joy of the angels, who consoled her and showed her the preparation for her future triumph. She also beheld the devils, but with little fear, for she was secure in her perfect union with God, which drives out all fear.

About four months before her death, after all the attempts of numerous physicians for her relief, another, more extraordinary, was made. Several medical men were summoned, who examined this suffering creature, investigated all the symptoms of her malady, and afterward came to the conclusion that it was supernatural, and no remedy of medical science could reach it. This she had often said herself, and refused to take the medicines prescribed her. But when the physicians persevered in their prescriptions, she took them in spirit of obedience, although with great pain and injury to herself, until the physicians themselves came to the above mentioned conclusion.

But there arrived from England a Genoese named Boerio, who had been for many years physician to the king of that country. He was surprised, when he heard of the fame of this holy lady, that she should speak of her infirmity as not natural

117

and requiring no medical remedy. Hardly believing this report to be true, he obtained permission to visit her, and reproved her for the scandal she caused by rejecting medical aid, even accusing her of hypocrisy. To all this she humbly answered: "It grieves me much to be the cause of scandal to any one, and if any remedy can be found for my disease, I am ready to make use of it." The physician, availing himself of her consent and obedience, applied various remedies, but at the end of twenty days, finding herself no better, she told him that she had submitted to his treatment in order to remove all scandal from his eyes, and from the eyes of others, but now he must leave the care of her soul to herself. For it was thus that the Holy Spirit (who worked and spoke through her) wished to confound the too great confidence of physicians in their science. After this Boerio held her in great reverence, calling her mother, and often visited her.

CHAPTER XL

*Of the many visions which the saint beheld in her last days.—Of
her acute sufferings.—How she could taste nothing but the
blessed sacrament, and suffered in herself the pains of the
passion of our Lord.*

During the last days of her life, her acute sufferings still
continuing, this blessed soul received impressions in accordance
with the divine operations in the saint whose day was celebrated.

On the evening of St. Lawrence's day her body appeared to
her in flames like his, and on the following day God visited her
by drawing her upwards, towards himself. She remained
immovable for more than an hour, with her eyes fixed on the
ceiling of her chamber. She did not speak, but often smiled in
sign of her interior joy. On returning to herself she told those
around, who questioned her, that the Lord had showed her one
spark of the joys of eternal life, and that her joy was so great that
she could not restrain her smiles, and repeated only these words:
"Lord, do with me all that seemeth good to thee," which showed
that the time was approaching when she was to pass from the
fires of purgatory into that blessed life. Her sufferings were
constantly increasing, followed by the sweetest consolation, until
the vigil of the Assumption, when they became so great that all
those around her believed her passing away to her Lord. When
she was about receiving communion, she addressed many
beautiful words to the holy sacrament, and to the persons
present: words of burning love from the interior fire of her heart,
so fervent and pious that every one wept with devotion.

The following day and the succeeding night she passed in
torture, and received extreme unction at her own request, with
great elevation. The next day she was in a state of such spiritual

joy, that it burst forth in her countenance, which was radiant with smiles, to the admiration of those who beheld it. When the vision had passed, she answered to their inquiries that she had seen some most beautiful countenances, beaming with joy, so that she could not contain her delight; but the impression remained with her for seven days, so that she appeared better. The cause was manifestly supernatural, the change from death to life taking place so suddenly, and then again her return continually to a worse condition, as she was drawing nearer to her end.

An attack so severe followed this vision that she lost the use of her left hand and side, and a finger of the other hand. She lay speechless for several hours, with her eyes closed, and could not swallow, though the persons about her attempted to give her nourishment; but the divine work going on within her was to be accomplished without human aid.

Her thirst was always so great that it seemed to her she could drink all the water of the sea, and yet she could not swallow the smallest drop, or take refreshment from any created thing. She would sometimes attempt to taste of fruit, but as soon as it touched her lips she rejected it.

On the night of the vigil of St. Bartholomew, she had a demoniacal vision, which threw her into great distress of body and mind. Being unable to speak, she motioned to have the sign of the cross made on her heart, and blessed herself; and by this it was understood that she was suffering from a temptation of the devil. She made a sign that a surplice, stole, and holy water should be brought her; this being done, in half an hour she was relieved. Oh! how wretched are those sinners who are carelessly awaiting this terrible presence, and a torment as terrible, it being so dreadful where there is no sin!

About the 25th of August, some liquid was offered her, which she took in obedience, but it caused her to scream from the distress it gave her. She afterwards fell into a state of great weakness, and asked to have the windows opened that she might see the sky. As night came on, she had a great many candles lighted, and then, as well as she could, she sang the Veni Creator Spiritus. When it was finished, she lay with her eyes upturned towards heaven, making signs, which led those about her to believe that she saw wonderful things.

Her countenance was radiant with joy, and she seemed just about to breathe her last; but recovering herself, she repeated again and again: "Let us go;" adding, "no more earth, no more earth." When questioned as to what she had seen, she answered that she could not describe those things, but they were very pleasant.

On the 27th of the same month, she seemed as if left without any life of her own, and resting with her spirit alone in God. She dismissed every one from her apartment, saying: "Let no one enter this room except those who are absolutely needed." She held no more conversation with creatures, except so far as necessity required, and when she had need of any service, she said only, "Do this in charity." This was contrary to her usual habit, for she was accustomed to speak always with entire confidence and frankness to every one; and always expressed great gratitude for any service done her. But at this time she could not look upon any service as done to herself, but only for the love of God. This state she continued in for two days.

On the 28th of August, the feast of St. Augustine, her sufferings were very great, and for some months before her death, she appeared to suffer much more on feast days, especially on those of our Lady, and of the apostles and martyrs. Often she cried aloud in her agony; but her silent sufferings were the greatest, when her tongue and lips were so parched with the burning fire within that she could not move them or speak. At such times if any one touched a hair of her head, or even the edge of the bed or the bed clothes, she would scream as if she had been wounded.

When she was unable to swallow the smallest morsel of food, or a drop of liquid, she could always receive holy communion; and sometimes when her confessor found her in such a state that he feared to give it to her, she would make a sign, with a joyful countenance, that she was not afraid, and often, on receiving her face was glowing and radiant with joy, like a seraph.

Sometimes she extended her arms as if stretched on the cross, and it seemed as if the stigmata were interiorly impressed on her, although they did not appear outwardly. On one occasion fresh water was brought her to cool her hands, and after bathing the palms, it became boiling hot, so as to heat even the stand of the cup, which had a very long stem. She also suffered greatly at this time in her feet.

As the burning fire within increased, her thoughts and imagination were filled with different sins, which she had never before thought of these, however, did not cause her any compunction but the remembrance of them gave her great pain. Her attendants, seeing her extreme weakness, and that she had not taken food for so long a time, on the 10th of the month of September assembled ten physicians, in order to ascertain if medical science could invent any remedy for her sufferings. After the most careful investigation of her case, they decided that her condition was produced wholly by supernatural causes, and was beyond the reach of medical skill, for all her bodily organs were in good order and showed no sign of infirmity; and they took their leave, lost in wonder and recommending themselves to her prayers.

On the 12th, she again received holy communion, but took no food; she also made a will naming the place in which she wished to be buried; then she lay alternately like one dead, motionless and speechless, or groaning with the internal flames that were consuming her and which raged so fiercely that black blood flowed from her mouth. Her body was covered with black stripes. After these attacks she became more and more exhausted, and on one occasion, having her eyes raised to the ceiling and fixed, she made so many signs to those around that

122

they inquired of her what she saw, and she answered, "Drive away that beast;" but they could understand nothing more.

CHAPTER XLI

In what manner, and at what time, she passed from this life to the Lord.—Many persons saw that blessed soul, under different forms, and in different ways, unite itself with God.—What happened to her confessor when he was celebrating the Mass of the Martyrs.

At length, on the 14th of September she had so violent a bleeding that her body seemed deprived of every drop of moisture. All the blood remaining within had been dried up by the fire that was consuming her. Her pulse was hardly perceptible, but her mind was clear. During the night she talked freely, and received communion as usual, continuing in the same state until seven o'clock on the following evening.

On Saturday night, as the morning of Sunday was approaching, she was asked if she wished to receive communion, to which she answered, "Not yet," when she found that it was not the usual hour. Then, raising the finger of her right hand to heaven, she wished, it would seem, to show that she was going to make her communion in heaven, there to unite herself wholly with her Love, and triumph with him forever; and, as hitherto she had been separated from all earthly things, seeing that her hour had now come, she knew that she should need no more communions on earth; and at that moment this blessed soul peacefully and gently expired, saying, "Into thy hands, O Lord, I commend my spirit," and took flight to her sweet and long-desired Love.

After her death that yellow tint which before was only seen about the region of the heart, diffused itself over her whole body, which signified that the divine fire had gradually consumed her whole humanity, which was preserved alive in the flesh until every, even the last particle was consumed; and then, free from every pain, she went forth from this purgatory, beatified, to take her place, as we must believe, in the choir of the Seraphim. For so purified was she by the divine fire in this life, it would seem that the Lord must have exalted her to such a glorious elevation.

This, her most happy transit, took place in the year 1510, on Saturday night, December 14th, as the hour of Sunday was approaching when she usually received communion. Among the persons present was one of her spiritual daughters, who saw the soul depart swiftly, and fly to God, without hindrance; and this sight gave her great consolation, and so much light, that she addressed those about her in words of burning love, exclaiming: "Oh! how narrow is the way by which we must pass, to arrive, without hindrance, at our home."

Another spiritual daughter of the saint, who, by divine permission, was tormented by an evil spirit, suffered dreadfully at that hour, and the spirit being forced to declare the cause, said that he had seen that soul unite herself with God.

Her faithful physician was asleep, and awoke as she departed, hearing a voice saying to him, "Rest in God, for I am now going to Paradise." At these words he called his wife, and told her that the Lady Catherine had died just at that moment, and it was found to be so.

Another person, who was praying, saw at the same hour Catherine ascending to heaven on a white cloud, and being very spiritual and devout, he experienced such joy and consolation at the sight, that he was like one beside himself, and although at a distance, he was as certain of her death and glory as if he had been present.

A holy, religious lady also saw her in her sleep, clothed in white, with a girdle about her waist. She told her companion that she had seen the soul of the blessed Catherine going to heaven, and in the morning, to her great joy, she found that it was so.

Another religious was at that hour rapt in spirit, and saw Catherine so beautiful, joyful, and content, that she believed herself in Paradise. She called her by her name, and told her many things which prepared her to suffer for the love of God, and determined her to change her life, which she did; and she was after heard to speak of the comfort she received from the memory of that vision.

It would be a long history to relate all the other persons who had the same vision, in various places, and under various circumstances. Her confessor had no notice of her death, on that night, nor the following: but the next day but one, happening to celebrate the mass for many martyrs, and not thinking, at the time, of that blessed soul, he had such a clear vision of her martyrdom, that he knew every word he uttered was appropriate to her sufferings; and his heart was so wounded with compassion and devotion, that he burst into tears, and was hardly able to continue the mass; but in the midst of his weeping he experienced great interior joy and satisfaction at the divine disposal and her repose.

All present at that mass—and they were friends of the blessed Catherine—could not restrain their weeping, so that the confessor himself was overwhelmed with astonishment, and could, with difficulty, finish the service. After it was concluded, he retired, and indulged his tears to relieve the oppression of his heart. So clearly was the great suffering of that chosen soul revealed to his mind, that all he had seen of it with his bodily eyes and known by long experience, seemed as nothing to the reality, and if God had not helped him, he would have died of grief.

CHAPTER XLII

Of her burial, and how the body was preserved in the midst of great moisture and putrefaction.—How many prayers were granted by her intercession, and a person restored to health.— Of the order she gave to have her heart opened, which was not done.

The body of this saint was interred in the principal hospital of the city of Genoa, in which, for many years, she had served the sick. It was first put in a beautiful wooden case, near the wall under which it was not noticed that an aqueduct passed. It remained there nearly a year, and when it was disinterred, the tow laid around the body was filled and covered with large worms that had been generated by the moisture produced by the water; but not one had touched the holy body, which was entire from head to foot, and the flesh dried rather than consumed.

Crowds of people flocked to see this wonderful sight, so that it was found necessary to expose it for eight days. But as some depredations had been committed on it, it was enclosed in a chapel where it might be seen and not touched. It caused great surprise when the cloths that wrapped it, and even the wood of the coffin, were seen to be destroyed and spoiled, and the body uncorrupted and without a stain.

Many were graciously heard who recommended themselves to her, and among others a friend of hers, who was sick, obtained the favor of restoration to health. Her infirmity confined her to her bed, but having had a vision of the happy state of the blessed soul, she directed that she should be carried into the church and placed near the body. On applying the cloths that were about it to the place where her pains were most severe, and commending herself to the saint, she was instantly cured, and returned to her house alone, without any assistance. For this great favor received, she caused a mass of our Lady to be offered at each anniversary, and another on the Festival of the Assumption, and left provision at her death that these masses should be perpetual.

At present the blessed Catherine is held in great devotion, in consideration of her holy life, illuminated with such peculiar graces. She directed, some months before her death, that her body should be opened and the heart examined, to see if it were not wholly consumed by love, yet her friends did not venture to do it.

That holy body was placed in a marble sepulcher, erected in the church of the hospital; but it was afterwards removed to a less conspicuous tomb, on account of the inconvenience caused by the number of persons coming to visit it.

It remains for us to pray our most merciful Lord, that by the intercession of this blessed soul, he may bestow on us the abundance of his love, that we may all advance from virtue to virtue, and at length be united in eternal bliss with Him who liveth and reigneth eternally.

SPIRITUAL DIALOGUE BETWEEN THE SOUL, THE BODY, SELF-LOVE, THE SPIRIT, HUMANITY, AND THE LORD GOD

In the first part St. Catherine relates in what manner she was captivated by worldly allurements, and how, from this state, she was entirely converted to God, and devoted herself to austere works of penance.

In the second, she describes the sublime perfection of the spiritual life in which she is engaged.

In the third, she discourses of the divine love and of its wonderful effects, and how she has experienced them all in herself.

FIRST PART

containing the discourse of the Soul with the Body and Self-Love; and also of the Spirit with Humanity

CHAPTER I

The soul and the body propose to travel in company, and to take self-love for a third party.

I saw, said the saint, a Soul and a Body conversing with one another; and first, the Soul said: My Body, God has created me to love, and to enjoy myself; I wish, therefore, to go where I can best accomplish this design, and to have you accompany me in a friendly way, since it will be to your advantage also. We will go through the world; if I find anything which pleases me, I will enjoy it; you can do the same when you find anything which pleases you; and let him do better that can.

The Body answered: Though I may be obliged to do whatever pleases you, yet I see that you cannot accomplish all that you wish without me. Therefore, if we are to set forth together let us come to a perfect understanding before we start, in order that we may not fall out by the way. For my own part, I agree to your proposal, but let each of us be satisfied with the success of the other when he meets with anything that pleases him, for such forbearance, will keep us in peace. I advise this beforehand, because I do not wish that you should deceive me, and say whenever I find something that I like: "I do not wish you to linger here, for I am going elsewhere to attend to my own concerns," and thus I might find myself obliged to abandon my own plans in order to follow yours. In that case, I assure you I should die, and our design would be frustrated. To prevent this, I think it would be well to take with us a third companion, some just person who has no share in our partnership, and to whom all our differences could be referred.

Soul. I am well-pleased with this proposal; but who shall this third person be?

Body. Let it be Self-Love, who lives with us both; he will see that I have what belongs to me, and I shall enjoy with him. He will do the same for you, and thus, both will be satisfied, each in his own way.

Soul. What shall we do if we find food equally gratifying to both?

Body. Let him eat who may. If there is enough for both there will be no disagreement. If there is not enough, Self-Love will give to each his share. But since our tastes are so different, it will be most extraordinary if we should find food equally pleasing to both, unless one or the other should change; which is contrary to the nature of things.

Soul. By nature I am more powerful than you, and therefore I have no fear of your converting me to your tastes.

Body. But this is my home, where I have so many delightful things to enjoy, that although you may be more powerful than I, you could not possibly awaken in me the desire to be converted to yours. But I, being, as I have said, at home, might more easily convert you to my tastes, doing it from love and from a wish to please you, for you are seeking things which you neither see, taste, nor understand,—nor do you even know where your home is.

Soul. Let us try the experiment; but, in the first place, we must make some agreement by which we may secure harmony. Let us take alternate weeks. When it is my turn you must do whatever is pleasing to me; and, in like manner, when yours comes, I will do whatever you wish, always excepting, so long as I live, whatever would offend our Creator. If I die, that is, if you induce me to offend him, I shall then be your servant to do your bidding, for in that case I shall be wholly converted to your wishes, and shall take pleasure in whatever pleases you. Being thus united, no one but God can ever interrupt our union, for it will always be protected by free-will; and both in this world and the next we shall receive together the reward of all the good and evil that we do. A like fate will be yours, if I succeed in conquering you.

But here comes Self-Love. You have heard the whole. Will you be our third party, our judge, and the companion of our journey?

Self-Love. I consent, and shall find it greatly to my advantage. I shall give each of you what belongs to him, for this will not injure me; and thus I shall live on equal terms with both. But if either of you should wrong me, and deprive me of my support, I shall immediately have recourse to the other, for on no account would I be deprived of my own subsistence.

Body. I am not one who would ever abandon you.

Soul. Nor would I ever do so, especially as we all agree and understand that, above all things, we are to avoid offending God. Therefore, if either of us sins, the others will check the offender. Now, in God's name, let us go, and I, being the most worthy, will take the first week.

Body. I am contented; guide me, and do with me whatever reason directs. Self-Love and I yield to you.

133

CHAPTER II

The Soul and the Body take their turns, in which each enjoys itself according to its wishes and tastes.

Then the Soul said within itself:

Soul. I, who am pure and without a stain of sin, will begin by considering my first creation and all the other benefits I have received from God. I know that I was created for such blessedness, and of such dignity, that I can almost soar above the choirs of angels, and I find myself in possession of a mind all but divine; for I am always drawn by my pure intelligence to the meditation and contemplation of divine things, and filled with the constant desire to eat my bread with the bread of angels. I am, in truth, invisible. I would have, then, all my food and all my delight in things invisible, for to this end was I created, and here I find my rest. I have nothing to do but to draw down from heaven the strength which I need, and to put all things else beneath my feet; I will, therefore, spend this entire week in contemplation, and take heed of naught else. Let him live thus who can do so; and he who cannot must have patience.

But I see that my companions are growing restless. I will go towards them. Well, my comrades, I have finished my week; do you, O Body! treat me in yours as you see fit. But tell me, how has it fared with you while I took my turn?

Self-Love. Not well; for into your regions neither Self-Love nor mortal Body can enter. We have had not the slightest nourishment and are nearly dead; now, however, we hope to have our revenge.

Body. Now it is my turn. Come, Soul, with me. I will show you how much God has done for me. Behold the heavens and the earth with all that adorns them; the sea with its fish, the air with its birds; and then, so many kingdoms, principalities, cities, provinces, as well spiritual as temporal: great dignities, numerous treasures; songs, sounds, and food of every kind for my support in never-failing supplies to the end of time, as well as innumerable other delights. And I can enjoy all these without offending God, for he created them all for me. You have not shown me your country as I am showing you mine. But as I cannot have my will unless you deign to indulge me in it, I venture to remind you that you are under great obligations to me, and that you must not think of going into that country of yours, and leaving me starving on the earth. You cannot do it, for I should die, and it would be your fault; you would offend God, and then we should all be your enemies. I have the advantage of being able to enjoy all these things while I live, and in the next life of enjoying your country also, saving myself, as I shall do, by your means. Remember that I am concerned in your salvation, for I shall be always with you; and do not believe that I desire anything contrary to reason, or displeasing to God. Ask your comrade, Self-Love, if I am not speaking the truth. I would not be unreasonable in my demands, and I will abide by his decision. I am sure that what I am seeking for you, is not only needful, but also agreeable to the will of God.

CHAPTER III

How Self-Love blames both the Soul and the Body, and wishes to rule them himself.—The Soul complains, and the Body, adhering to Self-Love, demands what its needs require.

Self-Love. I see your motives, which seem to me very reasonable when you do not go beyond the bounds of charity which God prescribed when he said: "Love thy neighbor as thyself." But, in the first place, the Soul has made no account of us, so that we have been actually in peril of our lives; and, on the other hand, I have seen the Body making too great a display to the Soul, of things that are unnecessary to both. In short, O Soul, you must restrain your impulses, and condescend to the necessities of your neighbors, your Body, and myself, if we undertake to live with you in that country of yours I have found nothing for myself; it is, in good truth, the very last of all places in which I should choose to take up my abode. As for you, O Body, it is enough for you to have the necessaries of life, since superfluities are as injurious to you as they would be to the Soul, were she to yield to you. But if you give them up, each of you will be able to live moderately, and according to his taste; I shall find it possible to remain with you, and being thus united, each will enjoy, with discretion, the advantages belonging to the others. If you wish, O Soul, to avail yourself of the Body, you must give it the requisite support, or it will complain; if you nourish it, it will be quiet, and you can use it as you please. In that case, both of you will be at peace, and I shall be obliged to go away, for I could not live with you. This is my opinion.

Soul. I am greatly displeased and dissatisfied to be obliged to condescend, in so many things, to the Body; and I fear that feeding it, under this plea of necessity, will lead to my taking part in its gratifications, and thus finally losing the greater for the less. Seeing both of you so craving, makes me fear that you will give me so much to do, that you will change me from spiritual into earthly; for, after tasting earthly things, I shall lose my relish for heavenly ones. I fear, too, lest the intellect should be defiled and the will corrupted. Help me, O my God!

Body. It seems to me that Self-Love has settled the question, and we may go on joyfully in company. As far as you are concerned, O Soul, do not forget that God would not have created the things that he has created, if they were injurious to souls. The Soul was endowed with so much power and dignity, that she cannot be held back without her own consent, for her will is so much respected by God that He never forces it. Neither I nor others, therefore, can take anything from you but by your own consent. You hold the reins; give to each what he needs, and then let him complain who will.

The Soul. What are these necessities of which you speak as indispensable? Tell me, that I may, once for all, provide for them, and never think of them again; the mere idea of them greatly disturbs me.

Body. I must have clothes, food, drink, and sleep; and be served, and amused, if you wish me to be in a condition to serve you when occasion requires; when you desire to occupy yourself with spiritual things, you must not weary me, for if I am taxed too much I shall not be able to attend to your affairs. But if you will look after my necessities, you can entertain your mind with the thought that God, who has made so many delightful things for this mortal body, has provided much greater goods for you, O immortal Soul! Thus God will ever be praised, and each of us be satisfied in his own way. If any difference occurs between us, our Self-Love, who is so wise, will adjust it, and we shall all be able to live together in most holy peace.

Soul. Come, then; I will provide for your necessities, since I cannot do otherwise; but I suspect that you have joined against me. Yet your words appear so reasonable that I am obliged to submit although I distrust you when I hear you so often refer to me, and say that you can do nothing without me. Perhaps, by the help of God, I shall one day escape your hands, and live in his service without you.

CHAPTER IV

The Soul, the Body, and Self-Love pursue their journey, during which the Soul cannot complete her whole week, and the Body encroaches upon it.—The Soul allows herself to be persuaded by Self-Love under pretext of the necessities of her two companions.—The Soul laments her condition and proposes not to take her turn again.

Body. Let us go straight forward on our journey, and thus traveling through the world in harmony, each will accomplish his own business, seeking, according to his condition, support, food, and pleasure.

Soul. My turn has come again, but alas! I cannot do as I did at first. I find myself drawn to earth by the pressing necessities of others, for which I am bound to provide; and thus my time passes only half-improved, while I live with these my companions on the best terms I can. It seems to me a heavy mortification to be obliged to leave so great a thing as divine contemplation, in order to employ myself in providing food for animals; so that the difference between this week and the other is as great as between light and darkness.

Body. This is my week, and I find myself almost famished through the fastings imposed upon me by the Soul. Yet I see that she condescends to my necessities, and therefore, I must take good care of myself and gain all the strength I can. Indeed I feel better already. In this way, I need not fear what the Soul may do to harm me during her week, especially as she is not able to keep the high stand she took at first, and thus I have not only my own week, but half of hers; and my needs, which she cannot but supply, are growing greater every day.

Soul. O Self-Love! I see that I am robbed of my rights by condescending to your endless necessities, and leaving the right path by permitting myself to be led by you, who are so self-seeking; in the end, we may find ourselves all astray. Will you, then, who are the umpire, tell me candidly what you think?

Self-Love. Soul, you have, without any cause, become so estranged from us, that you think it a great matter to condescend to the needs of others, especially from the height to which you had ascended. By degrees, however, you will become more settled; and keeping company with us will not appear so great a hardship to you as it now does. Have no doubts—God will provide. You are not to enjoy perfect happiness in this life, but in the next. Now take what you can get, and do the best you can.

Soul. I see not how I can defend myself, since I live with you, and you are united against me. It does me no good to take my turn, for your wants are so incessant that you allow me not a day's rest, and so engrossing that I have no time for myself.

And when your turn comes, you wish to have everything according to your own pleasure and proclaim yourselves masters. I cannot but be a loser in the end, and therefore, I think seriously that I will try this plan no longer, but will let each one provide for himself, and find food where he can. I shall try to bear myself toward each of you in the best way I am able, since I have no choice in the matter, but must, perforce, remain with you.

Body and Self-Love. In our judgment this will answer very well. We can all live peaceably without quitting our own spheres, the more easily, since you, O Soul! have at length discovered your mistake.

CHAPTER V

The Soul yields to the allurements of the Body and of Self-Love, and falls into the depths of sin.—Of the little satisfaction she takes in earthly things, and the trifles that are sufficient to content the Body.—Of the troubles of the Soul.

And thus they went traveling through the world, each seeking to gratify his own desires, and living according to his own pleasure. The Soul looked after the Body, and granted it many things that it esteemed necessary; but, day by day, its appetites increased, incited by Self-Love, which bound them closely together, that they might not become divided. Everything appeared to them reasonable and necessary. They were never willing to deny themselves anything, and if they were not permitted to obtain every day something new, some fresh nourishment, they murmured, and complained that they were injured. Thus was the Soul finally led into an unfathomable sea of earthly love and delight, which effected in her so great a transformation, that she could no longer think or speak of anything, except according to the will of the Body and Self-Love. If she wished to turn to her own concerns, overpowered by her disorderly appetites, she dared not speak; and, in her discontent, she thus reflected within herself:

"If they should lead me as far into their own country as I led them into mine, during the first week, who will rescue me from their power? Without doubt, they will, under the plea of necessity, do with me whatever they see fit."

Now this Soul, which still craved some support for her life, in order not to fall into despondency, as she had been created for love and happiness, trimmed her sail to the wind, although it was contrary, and finding herself no longer able to live in her own region, she still sustained herself, as best she could, saying, with some show of truth: "This beauty, pleasure, goodness, grandeur, and delight, together with all that adorns created things, furnish one means of knowing and tasting those that are divine;" and when she had tasted them she exclaimed: "Oh, how beautiful must be celestial things!"

And thus, still traveling with her two companions, she daily lost something of her natural, divine instinct, and fed on the husks for swine, as bestial as the body, so that, in a short time, the three found themselves on very good terms with one another.

While they were journeying on, in such great love and harmony, without any dissension, we may imagine what became of the rights of the superior reason. Nothing more was said about it. All their attention was turned to earthly things, to temporal pleasures, delights, and loves; and spiritual things seemed so unpalatable to them that they had no desire either to speak or hear of them, lest they should interfere with their earthly satisfactions. Thus they continued for some time, until nothing remained to the soul but a little compunction, which she seldom noticed, although at times she did so when it remained her of the risk she ran of losing everything at death. This thought caused her great fear, but when it left her she returned to the same course as before. One thing alone was against her, and that was, that although her companions and herself were all agreed to satisfy their appetites as fully as possible, yet they were not able to do so; for the soul having a boundless capacity, all finite and earthly things could neither satisfy her nor give her peace; the more she sought, the more restless she became, because she wandered farther every day from God, her true rest.

Yet earthly things so far blinded her that she believed she found peace here below; she strove, therefore, to keep herself continually occupied, in order to satisfy herself, and when she could not accomplish this in the manner she proposed, she became disgusted, and, in her interior blindness, tried something else. Thus passing from one thing to another, and from one hope to another, she forgot herself; and losing her time in these pursuits, she never obtained her wish, for so it was mercifully ordained by the Lord God. And certainly if man could find rest on earth, few souls would be saved, for they would become so absorbed in earthly things that they would make no effort to free themselves from them. The Soul, by her natural instinct, seeks enjoyment; and when she is blinded by the Body, she procures her pleasures through its means. So the Body leads her on from one thing to another, as they seek their food together; and though the Soul has an infinite capacity, and cannot, by means of the Body, find aught that will content her, yet she foolishly allows herself to be led by it, without receiving any satisfaction.

But the more the Body assimilates the Soul to itself, the more ways has it to enjoy and please itself with earthly things, since all its satisfaction comes through the condescension of the Soul; so that, if the Soul did not give her consent, the Body would have neither enjoyment nor delight. But as the Body is so closely united with the Soul, which cannot be contented with the things of earth, and as it cannot further her wishes, nor yield her the enjoyment she desires, therefore she is famished. And this is because the tastes of the Body are capable of satisfaction; for when its wants, of whatever nature, are appeased, the appetite is lost, and it can enjoy no more. It is true that it does not lose the desire to seek new pleasures in accordance with its natural tastes, but it can find nothing to satisfy it entirely; not, indeed, that the Soul will not condescend, nor that the health of the Body will not permit, but only because it has gone to the limit of its capacity, and hence both Soul and Body are ill at ease.

The Soul is disquieted because she finds herself in this vessel of the Body, so narrow and requiring so little to replenish it, although whenever it is empty, all created things seem insufficient to fill it. She is obliged to remain in it, although she is well nigh famished while urged on by her natural instinct for enjoyment. This happens by reason of the sympathy of the Soul when she wishes to procure enjoyment by means of the Body, for when she finds that the Body is satisfied with a trifle, and

143

that it cannot further indulge itself because its desires are blunted, she is distressed by this, and also, because she cannot herself enjoy what still remains to be enjoyed. The more she gratifies her tastes, the less enjoyment she obtains from them; for it is in vain that man strives to regain his lost appetites, since he endangers his life thereby. Therefore the Soul addresses Self-Love, in the following words:

CHAPTER VI

How the Soul discourses further with Self-Love, proposing a new mode of action.—Of the nature of Self-Love.—Of the little required to satisfy the desires of the Body.—How the Soul falls into misery and despair.

Soul. O Self-Love! do you not see how we molest each other, and how ill-fed we are? You have made me yield to your appetites, and now I am wretched indeed. I no longer pasture in heaven, and you starve me to death on earth: how is it with you?

Self-Love. I see that you are both dissatisfied, and thus far, not without reason. Let us go on, however, and perhaps we shall, by and by, find upon the road some good that may suit us all. I see plainly that this Body can consume but little, so that I, too, am not supplied with all the nourishment I am capable of taking. In one instant I devour what would satisfy the Body for a year, and how must it be then with you, whose capacity so far exceeds mine? This we will go: let us go in search of food better suited to us than we have hitherto found, give the Body as much of it as it requires (which is a trifle when compared to our needs), and then let it complain as much as it likes.

Soul. On what do you nourish yourself, and what can we find that will satisfy us both, and yet sustain the Body?

Self-Love. I have a great appetite; I feed both on earthly and on spiritual food; but do not take me to that place where you went the first week, but rather to any other spot. When I travel with any one and find enough to live upon, I seldom abandon my company; I collect such supplies that my followers are never in want, and I make them all rich.

Soul. I know that there is not on earth food suited to us both, from the fact that there is not enough to satisfy us. We have wandered so far from heaven (where there is food in plenty) that I know and can find no way that will lead us thither again; and I see that God closed the door of this grace at the moment when we deliberated whether we should feed according to the tastes of his world, and has left us to gratify our appetites. Now that we are perplexed and discouraged about our pasturage, we wish to return to him for our own benefit, and not through true and pure charity, which the Lord requires from us, and by which he always works in us. When I think of all I have done for you, and of all that I have justly lost, I see that I deserve to be abhorred by God, by you, by the world, and by hell. I am almost in despair through shame at finding myself led by you into the midst of earthly things, in which I believed I could find a supply for our joint necessities, while we remained together in this world. But, after trying everything, I find that not one of us could be contented or satisfied even if we had all we asked on earth. I have witnessed and proved all your appetites, and I have found that your way of quieting them greatly inflamed them; and yet, that they are so quickly satiated that after even a little gratification they were disordered, although there had been such an intense craving for that little. Yet, though blunted, they were never appeased. They were always finding themselves in the same condition. When they seemed satisfied I was famishing; and when I wished to return to my own country, to gratify my instincts, I found no cooperation as at first, for I had withdrawn from my first path, which was straight, clear, and open for all spiritual operations. Having consented to this, by reason of certain disorders of the Body, under the plea of supposed necessity, at once superfluity followed in the train of necessity, and shortly I was buried in sin; and in this snare I lost grace, became blind and dull; and from spiritual, wholly earthly. Now, alas! I am in such a condition that I can only move earthward, whereby I am drawn into every evil, like one who has wandered from his home. I leave myself to be led by you, O Body and Self-Love, wherever it pleases you, and you have carried me so far that I cannot even resist your appetites.

You have, by degrees, so changed me, or I might rather say, perverted me, that I feed on the same food as yourselves; and we are so united and agree so well, that I blindly fall in with all your desires, and have, thus, from a spiritual soul become almost an earthly body. And you, Self-Love, are so closely bound to us, and keep us so closely bound to each other, that I, poor creature, am like one chained and stifled, and, as it were, dead to spiritual things. As if deprived of interior light and taste, I go on, gazing at and tasting things earthly and corporeal, and there is no good thing remaining to me, except a certain secret remorse which leaves me but little rest. Yet I continue neglecting myself, and enjoying, as I may, these earthly things which I feed upon, and wasting my time, while daily I bring myself into greater slavery; and the farther I withdraw from God, the more dissatisfied am I with my estrangement from my natural good, which is God himself.

Thus did this unhappy Soul often bewail her wretchedness, while yet she was ignorant of its cause. This was the divine instinct which she naturally possessed; for the all-merciful God never abandons one of his creatures while it remains in this life, but often visits it with some inspiration, by which man finds himself aided when he listens to it, although, if he resists it, he often becomes worse, by reason of his ungrateful neglect of preventing grace.

This unhappy Soul soon became so burdened with sins and ingratitude, with no visible remedy, that she lost all hope of being delivered from them, and went so far as not only to take pleasure in sin, but even to boast of it. The greater were the graces she had received, so much the greater was her blindness of heart and her despair of doing right; so that it was impossible that, by any human means, she should ever obtain relief. Nothing remained but that God should rescue her by his infinite grace and goodness; for she had now fallen so low that all her desires, affections, interests, and delights, were fixed upon earthly objects. Everything else she hated and never mentioned, for she was so perverted that what once seemed sweet to her, now appeared very bitter, through the change of her taste from heavenly to earthly.

CHAPTER VII

Of the light which God gave to the Soul to discover all her
faults, and the state into which she had sunk.—Of her
submission, confidence, and conversion.

After God in his goodness had left the Soul to wander for
awhile among the things of this world until she became
disgusted (for she soon found by experience that such things
could never satisfy her; but that, on the contrary, they became
daily more distasteful), this merciful God sent a light which
penetrated her intellect, and showed her all the errors and
dangers into which she had fallen, and from which God alone
could deliver her. When she saw just where she was, and what
path she was pursuing, and that the death of the body was on one
side, and the death of the soul on the other, and found herself in
the midst of so many enemies whom she allowed to lead her like
a beast to the shambles, and even seemed to go joyfully on her
way, terror seized upon her and with a deep and piteous sigh she
turned to God, and cried to him as best she could.

Soul. O wretched creature that I am! who will deliver me
from all this misery? God alone is able: Domine, fac ut videam
lumen, that I may escape these snares.

No sooner had she directed her thoughts to God, and
implored his help, without which she saw she had no power to
move, but could only go from bad to worse, than suddenly her
confidence in him became firm, and she left him to do his own
will in what manner, and so far as it pleased him; and she added:

Soul. From henceforth all that befalls me I will receive as
from the benign hand of God, excepting my sins, for they are all
my own; committing them is always contrary to the divine will,

and therefore they are our own property; nothing is ours but voluntary sin.

This firm resolution, made by the Soul before God, was secret and in her own spirit alone, without any outward demonstration. Now, when God sees that man distrusts himself, and places his whole confidence in Providence, he immediately stretches forth his holy hand to help him. He stands ever at our side, he knocks, and, if we open to him, he enters; he drives forth our enemies one after another, and restores to the Soul its baptismal robe of innocence; and all this God does in different modes and ways, operating according to the state in which he finds his creature. For the present we will speak of his dealings with Self-Love, and how he purifies the soul from it.

CHAPTER VIII

Of many illuminations received by the Soul, and of the pure love of God.—Of conscience, and the remorse which God awakens in it.

When God wills to purify a soul from self-love, he first sends her his divine light, that by it she may discern a spark of that pure love wherewith he loves her, and how much he has done and still does by means of this love; for he has need of us in nothing, not even the least thing. We are his enemies, not only by our nature, which is inclined to evil, but by our manifold offences, which we are ever ready to repeat.

He also discovers to her that our sins can never excite his anger so far that he ceases to do us good while we are in this world; rather does it seem that the more our sins remove us from him, so much the more does he seek to draw us toward himself by many incentives and inspirations, in order that his continued love and his benefits may keep us still in his love. The better to effect this, he uses countless ways and means, so that every soul, beholding what he has done for her, may exclaim, full of admiration: "What am I that God seems truly to have no care for any one but me?"

And, among other things, he discovers to her that pure love with which he created us, and how he requires nothing of us but that we should love him with that same love wherewith he has loved us, and that we should remain ever with him, expecting no return except that he may unite himself to us.

And he shows her how this love was chiefly proved in the pure angelic creation, and afterwards in that of our father Adam, created in his purity and sincerity by that divine love of his, wherewith God desired to be loved and obeyed; for if he had not required submission in something from Adam and his posterity, such was the excellence in which they were created that each one could have believed himself a god, by reason of the rare gifts bestowed on both the body and the soul, and of the dominion given him over all created things; but God placed him under a slight restraint only, in order that he might ever know his Maker, and render him obedience.

God, moreover, made known to this Soul that he had created man for the highest good, namely, that with soul and body he might enter into his heavenly home.

He also showed her how great an evil is sin, into which she had herself fallen, and for which there was no remedy but another manifestation of his love, which he was obliged to make in her behalf. And he further instructed her in that ardent love for us of which our Lord Jesus Christ gave such proof on the earth, from the Incarnation even unto the Ascension, and all to save us from eternal damnation.

All this did God, by his most pure act, reveal in an instant to the Soul.

She then saw the liberty in which he had created her, not subjecting her to any creature, but to her Creator alone; for he had given her free-will, over which, while she remains in this world, nothing on earth or in heaven has any power.

He allowed her to see the great patience with which he had waited for her, and borne with so many of her sins, in which, if she had died, she would have been lost forever.

He reminded her how often she had been in danger of death; and how, through pure love alone, he had rescued her, that she might have time to know her error and escape eternal damnation.

He also reminded her of the many inspirations he had given her to save her from sin, and although she had not only disregarded, but even gone contrary to his will, yet in his goodness, he did not cease to send them, now in one way, now in another, and so allured her free-will, that he had, as it were, forced her to do that which in his goodness he required. And this, too, he did so gently and patiently, that no example of human love was ever known on earth, which could compare with it.

God also made known to this Soul that, by reason of the great love he bears him, his anger is never inflamed against man, but that he always loves him, and is ever seeking to unite him to himself in love; and that on his side this instinct never fails, so that his pure love, which ever burns yet never consumes, is always active on our behalf, and he shows himself terrible only toward sin. Moreover he hates nothing but sin, which alone prevents his love from doing its work in us; for even the devils, if it were not for the heinousness of their sins, would burn with divine love.

God made plain to her, also, how he is always waiting to inflame and penetrate the hearts of men with burning rays of love, and how he is thwarted by sin. Therefore, if sin is taken away, all things are in peace; where sin is, there is never aught but strife.

She saw, likewise, the love of God for man, which, however great a sinner he may be, is never so entirely extinguished as not to bear with him while life lasts; beyond that, all is hatred and never-ending wrath.

She saw, too, a ray of his mercy shining into hell; for the wicked deserve infinite punishment for an infinite time; but the divine mercy has made the time only infinite, but has limited the extent of the punishment, and therefore a greater one might justly have been inflicted.

This Soul also beheld a certain ray of love issuing from that divine fountain, and darting towards man with a force as if to annihilate him; and she saw that when it found impediments, then, if it were possible for God to feel pain, he would suffer the greatest of all grief. This ray aimed only to penetrate the soul, and it was her own fault if she were not penetrated by it, for the ray surrounded her on all sides, seeking entrance; but the soul, blinded by self-love, did not perceive it. And when God saw a soul self-condemned, who through her willfulness would not give entrance to the light, he seemed to say: "So great is the love which I bear to this soul, that I desire never to abandon her."

This is because the Soul, deprived of divine love, becomes almost as malignant as the divine love is good and gracious: I say, almost, for God still grants it a little mercy. She heard these words, also: "So great is the love I bear thee, that I would never willingly see thee lost; gladly would I suffer for thee, if I could, but love and evil cannot dwell together, and therefore I must abandon thee; and as through me thou wouldst have become capable of all blessedness, so, abandoned by me, thou wilt be capable of all wickedness." So many operations and effects of love were shown to this Soul, that words fail to narrate them.

Touched by this ray, the Soul saw and felt a certain flame of love proceeding from that divine source, which, for the moment, left her like one bereft of sense, without understanding, without speech, without feeling. In that pure and simple love, as God manifested it to her, she remained at that moment wholly absorbed, and never more did this sight depart from her memory; always she beheld that pure, divine love turned toward her.

She was then shown how she had lived without the knowledge of this great love, and how great were the faults in which she saw herself, and what she could do to correspond to this pure love; and so humbled was she in her own eyes that she would have publicly proclaimed her sins through the whole city, and could do nothing but incessantly repeat these words: "O Lord! no more world, no more sin," with a cry of inward anguish which came from the depths of her heart.

But all that she beheld did not prevent the other vision of that first love infused by the ray from doing its work within her; so that her mind was lost in that pure love in which she saw all things, especially those imperfections which were to be removed. Yet she did not estimate her sins according to the punishment they merited, but rather as committed against the great mercy of God, for she saw his pure love for the Soul, and it remained always in her heart, continually drawing her towards God, from whom it descended. This love so melted her that all her actions were done with that purity which now dwelt in her; and she continued so united with that ray, that nothing inferior to God could come between that light and the soul, either as to the will or its effects.

CHAPTER IX

*The Soul speaks to Self-Love and the Body of the truth she had
seen, and tells them that she should be lost if she followed
them.—She warns them of her purpose to do to them what they
had designed to do to her, namely, to subject them to herself.—
Of the disgust they felt at this.*

After the Soul had seen the many things so skillfully, purely,
and carefully wrought in her by love she paused, and said to the
Body and Self-Love:

Soul. My brothers, I have come to know that God is about to
do a work of love on my behalf and therefore I shall take no
more heed of you, your needs, or your words, for I surely know
that if I heed you I shall perish, although I would never have
believed it, if I had not experienced it. Under the appearance of
good and necessity, you have wellnigh led me to the death of
sin, and have done all you could to bring me to perdition. Now I
intend to do to you what you have wished to do to me, and I
shall hold you in no more respect than if you were my deadly
enemies. Never expect to be on good terms with me again,—
give up all hopes of it as if you were among the lost. I shall
strive to return to that path which I first entered, and from which
you caused me to swerve by your deceits. I hope, however,
through the divine light, that you will deceive me no more, and
in the meanwhile I shall do all things in such a manner, that the
necessities of each will be satisfied. If you have led me to do
what I ought not, in order to satisfy your appetites, I will lead
you to what you do not desire, in order to satisfy the spirit. I
shall not spare you, even if you are worn out, even as you spared
me not when I was so enslaved by you, that you did with me

according to your pleasure. I hope to bring you into such subjection to myself as to change your natures.

The Body and Self-Love were greatly displeased when they found that the Soul had received so much light that they could no longer deceive her.

Body and Self-Love. We are subject to you, O Soul! let justice be done, and be the rest according to your pleasure. If we cannot subsist in any other way, we can live by violence; that is, you will oppose us as much as you can, and we will do all we can to injure you, and in the end each will be rewarded according to his deserts.

Soul. I will say one thing for your consolation: for a time you will be greatly dissatisfied, but when I have deprived you of your superfluities (which will distress you very much), you will be satisfied with all I have said and done, and you will participate forever in my welfare; dispose yourselves, therefore, to patience, for in the end we shall all enter into the divine peace. At present I will supply your necessities only, but afterwards you will have everything you desire. I will lead you to a joy so great and so secure, that you will wish for nothing more even in this life. Hitherto you have had nothing whatever in which you could take any satisfaction, and now, having tried all things, I hope to bring you to a place of the greatest happiness, which will have no end. It will begin, and go on increasing, until at length there will be such peace in the soul that the body too will feel it, and it will be enough to mitigate the suffering not alone of one, but of a thousand hells. Before this can be attained, much remains to be done, but (with light and help from God), we shall come out safely on every side; let this suffice for your encouragement. Henceforth I shall not speak, but act.

Body. You appear so terrible to me, and have made so deliberate an attack on me, that I fear you will go to some excess, to the injury of us all. I wish, therefore, to recall some things to your remembrance, and discourse with you concerning them, and then I will leave you to act your own pleasure. I would remind you that after the love of God, comes the love of the neighbor, which begins with one's own body and its concerns, and you are bound to preserve it not only in life but in health. If you fail to do so, you cannot succeed in your designs. I am necessary to your existence, for when I am dead, you will have no means of adding to your glory, nor time to purify yourself from all your imperfections, and purgatory must do this for you. That kind of penance you will find very different from bearing with a body in this world. As to health, when the body is sound, the powers of the soul and the bodily senses are in a better state to receive divine light and inspiration, even through the sense of taste, which, in the soul's esteem, passes for a superfluity. Now, if I am infirm, these things and many others that I could name would fail you, even as time fails me to enumerate them. I have said to you what seems to me most important both for your interest and mine that each may have his due, and both reach the port of salvation, without reproach in heaven or on earth.

Soul. I am made aware of all that is needful to me, interiorly by the divine light, and exteriorly by your reasons, and many more that might be thought of. But, henceforth, let me hear no more reasoning, or external persuasions, for I wish to give my attention to superior considerations, which are of such a sort that they can do injustice to no one, but will rather give to each all that he needs, so that none can complain, except of his own imperfections. Whoever complains, shows that he is not yet well-ordered, and that his appetites are not in subjection to reason. Leave all this to me, O Body, and I will make you change your opinion. You shall live in such content that you could never believe it, did you not experience it.

I was once mistress, when I first turned my thoughts to spiritual things; but afterwards I was deluded into making myself your equal, and we made with Self-Love a compact to do good, but only in such a manner that one should not take advantage of the other; by degrees, however, you so contrived that I became completely enslaved, and could do nothing but what was pleasing to you. Now, I am determined to be mistress again, with this understanding, that if you are willing to become my servant, I shall be contented, and you shall want for nothing that a servant needs. But if you will not be my servant, I shall compel you to become my slave, and so completely my slave, that you will be willing to serve me for love, and thus will all our opposition end, for in every way I will be served, and will be mistress.

CHAPTER X

Of the view which the Soul has of the goodness and providence
of God.—Of her faults and imperfections.—Of her esteem of
herself and hatred of her Humanity.

And thus this enlightened Soul began to see all her
irregularities and the perils, both of the spirit and the flesh,
which she had unawares encountered, and to which she would
have fallen a victim, had not the divine Providence interposed.
She was overwhelmed with astonishment at the great mercy of
God towards a being so deeply plunged in sin. But when man
begins to see the goodness and providence of God, then God
shows him also all his defects, for which he will supply the
remedy, and the soul perceives them in an instant by that divine
light, the light of pure love. The Soul, having these two clear
views, so definite and precise, the one of the goodness of God in
his bounty, granted in virtue of love, and the other of herself,
plunged in sins, and voluntarily acting in opposition to the
infinite goodness of God, took thought and said:

Soul. O Lord! never more will I offend thee, nor do anything
in opposition to thy goodness; for this thy great goodness has so
overpowered me and drawn me so closely unto thee, that I have
resolved never more to withdraw from thy disposal, even should
it cost life itself.

Then this Soul looked within, and seeing all her defects and
evil instincts, said:

Soul. Does it seem to you that you are prepared to present
yourself before your Maker? How is it with you? Who will
deliver you from all your difficulties? Now you see how
wretched and vile you are, although you believed yourself so
beautiful and good. And this happened because you were so

blinded by Self-Love, that you believed in no other paradise than that of sensual delights. And now, behold how all these things appear in the divine presence—truly no better than the work of the devil!

Then this Soul turned with a deep and bitter hatred toward Humanity, and said:

Soul. I warn you, O Humanity! that if henceforth you speak to me of aught unseemly, you shall suffer for it. For the future, I shall treat you as if you were an evil spirit, for you have ever been, and ever will be, diabolical in your behavior, since nothing else is known to you. And as you now see as well as I what a terrible thing it is to offend God, I know not how you will ever have the courage to think or speak according to your own natural appetites, when you know that you are thereby acting contrary to his will; however, should you do so, I shall inflict a penance upon you that you will not speedily forget.

When Humanity heard the Soul utter these words, and became conscious of the greatness of her offences, she answered not a word, but stood with downcast looks, like a criminal led to justice.

CHAPTER XI

*How the Soul turns to God and perceives her own sinfulness,
and also what she would have become had she continued her
former course.—Almost in despair she bewails her offences.—Of
the confidence with which our Lord inspires her, appearing to
her spirit; and of the wound she receives.*

The Soul then turned towards God, and in that clear light
spoke thus:

Soul. O Master! what has moved thee to give such light to
this Soul, so blind and so corrupt, thy enemy, who goes astray
from thee, ever feeding upon sensual things, and who is so
unwilling to be lifted out of that condition, that she always shuns
whatever would elevate her? I am stupefied when I consider
myself—a creature so entirely vile!

And while in this condition it was given her to see where she
was, whither she was going, what would have been her end, and
what she would have carried with her to that end had she
persevered in her course. She saw at a glance all these things as
they were, and as they would have been if God had not
interposed. At which sight she was beside herself with fear and
agitation, and could do nothing but weep, and sigh, and inwardly
lament, thus bewailing her sad condition:

Soul. Oh, wretched and most miserable! had I continued in
this course, how many trials and sorrows should I have brought
upon myself in this world; and in the next have found myself the
enemy of God, and condemned eternally to hell!

For a time this vision remained with her, and caused her such
interior suffering that she could neither think of other things nor
perform any cheerful action, but remained in a settled
melancholy, and knew not what to do with herself, for she could

find no rest; neither in heaven, which had no place for such as she, nor on earth, for she merited that it should swallow her up; nor did she feel that she had a right to appear among men, or to take heed of aught that concerned her comfort or discomfort. She saw that she alone had done all the evil, and earnestly desired that alone, and without help from any other creature, she might make satisfaction to the extent of her power; and for this reason she said:

Soul. I see that hell is my place, but I cannot reach it except through death. Alas! my God! what will become of me? I know not where to hide myself: I wander on, lamenting, and find no place of rest, for I am so stained with sin that I cannot appear where thou art, and yet I find thee everywhere. In this condition I am insupportable to myself. What, then, shall I do with this foul and tattered garment in which I find myself clothed? Tears are useless, sighs do not help me, contrition is not accepted, penances are fruitless; for nothing will satisfy for my sins if God will not be merciful and come to my assistance.

Thus the Soul remained almost in despair, powerless to make satisfaction, unable to have recourse to the mercy of God (for she found in herself nothing which could give her confidence, yet was not able wholly to despair), tormented within herself at the sight of the heavy burden which she carried, in agony of spirit at the evil she had done; she grieved interiorly, yet was unable to shed a tear, only heaving secret sighs which wellnigh consumed her life. She could neither speak, eat, sleep, smile, nor look up to heaven. She had neither spiritual nor natural feeling; nor did she know where she was, whether in heaven or on earth, but was like one stunned and senseless; gladly would she have hidden herself that she might not be found, nor be obliged to enter into the company of others.

So abstracted was she, and lost in this vision of the offended God, that she no longer seemed a rational creature, but like a frightened animal. And this happened because it was given her to see the greatness of her sins and the ruin that they caused—a sight which, had she beheld it longer, would have consumed her body had it been adamant.

But when God had left her to contemplate it until the impression could never be forgotten, he came to her assistance as we shall here relate.

One day in her dwelling our Lord Jesus Christ appeared to her interior vision, bleeding from head to foot, so that the blood seemed pouring in a stream from his body as he passed; and in secret she heard these words: "Seest thou this blood? it is shed for love of thee, and in satisfaction for they sins." At these words she was pierced with a deep wound of love for him, our Lord Jesus Christ, and at the same time her confidence returned and banished her despair, so that she began to rejoice a little in our Lord.

CHAPTER XII

How God once more manifested to the Soul the love with which he had suffered for her.—She sees the malice of man and the pure love of God.—Of the offering, which she makes of herself to God, and of the wound she receives.—Of the five fountains of Jesus.—Of his constant and jealous watchfulness.

Another sight was shown her, greater than the first, so much greater that no tongue could describe, nor intellect imagine it, and it was this: God showed her the love with which he had suffered for love of her. When the Soul saw this most pure and strong love wherewith God loved her, she was pierced with a wound so deep, so keen, that it made her despise every other love and everything that could interpose between herself and God, except it were God himself. In the light of this love she saw the malignity of man and the benignity of the pure love of God. These two visions never again faded away from her memory, and the one revealed to her the other; for, beholding the infinite mercy of God performing such works of pure love towards man, the Soul would have fainted from excess of delight if any more had been manifested to her. Such a vision, moreover, made clear to her the malice of man, seeing that great love of God continually employed in her behalf, almost, as it were, in spite of herself; for God, looking not at the sins that she committed, never ceased in his mercy to do her good in many ways, being moved by none of her offences but rather with pure love repairing them, always watchful for her benefit. Hereupon the Soul, turning towards herself, saw how sinful she had been in acting in opposition to the great goodness of God. And then she began to see the nature of man, with all his malice, as bad almost as God is good. But at this sight she fell into despair of herself, for man seemed to her the demon, with all his malignity; and if God had not in part veiled the sight, both Soul and Body would have fainted with fear. Hence as at the former vision of the divine love towards man she despaired within herself, as believing it to be irremediable, and wishing to lose no more time in seeking for a remedy, she turned, as her sole confidence, to God, her Love, and said to him:

Soul. Lord! I give myself to thee. I know not what I am fitted for but to make a hell by myself alone. O Lord! I desire to make this compact with thee: I will give this sinful being of mine into thy hands, for thou alone canst hide it in thy mercy, and so dispose of me that nothing of myself can any more be seen. Occupy me wholly with thy love, which will enlighten in me every other love and keep me wholly lost in thee, holding me so engrossed by thee that I shall find neither time nor place for self.

Her most sweet Lord made answer that he was content, and from that moment all thought and memory of self was lost, so that it never more disturbed her peace. On the other hand, a ray of love so burning and penetrating was infused into her heart and wounded her so deeply that in an instant it bereft her of every attachment, appetite, delectation, and natural quality that ever did or ever could belong to her. She was shorn of everything, though not without her own consent, by virtue of her correspondence with the love revealed to her, and by this she was so powerfully drawn that it astonished, absorbed, and transformed her. She sighed and lamented far more than when she beheld what a sinful creature she was.

This ray of love passed into her soul with the impression of the five wounds of Christ, as five fountains from which were flowing forth drops of blood and burning love for man. God gave her also the power to discern readily the nature of man; and she beheld alternately the one sight and then the other, so far as she could look upon them then the other, so far as she could look upon them and live. The sight of herself caused her no suffering, for her merciful God had relieved her of all sorrow on that account, and yet she saw herself plainly, and in what manner she was upheld by God. If ever God had left her to herself, she comprehended that she would have been ready to fall into all manner of wrong doing, for she saw herself as perverse as the evil spirit himself; but, finding herself in the hands of God, it was not possible in such good hands to feel any fear.

But the sight that tortured and consumed her was of that burning, divine love towards man; she said that no human tongue could describe how inflamed she was with that glowing fire. The love that God manifested to her made her instinctively reject whatever was displeasing to him, with a jealous watchfulness against the least defect; and her eyes were opened not to her sins only, but to her slightest imperfections and unnecessary practices. She heeded not the world, the flesh, nor the devil. All the devils who opposed her were not so strong as this soul in her union with God, who is the true strength of those who fear, love, and serve him; and so much the more because she did not perceive how she could be injured by self, it being in the hands of God and upheld by his goodness.

Chapter XIII

Of the instinct which led her to cast off every superfluous thing, and even that appear necessary.—Of her instinct for prayer and her mortification.

An instinct was given her to despise herself, and to hold everything under heaven in no more esteem than if for her it did not exist. This love gave her the further instinct to deny the body not only all superfluous food but also many things that appeared needful, and the same with regard to clothing, and all society, whether good or bad. She was led into solitude of mind and body, and was reduced to herself alone. An instinct for prayer was also given her, so that she would have remained for hours together, on her bare knees, to the great discomfort of Humanity, which, although it resented and disapproved of this, did not refuse to serve the Soul, and to follow wherever she led.

All these instincts were called into action by God alone, for the Soul had no wish or aim but God, who had taken the direction, and wished to regulate all her desires and inclinations, and free her from all those that were human and worldly by giving her contrary ones. She was deprived of the use of fruits for which she had a natural inclination and an especial fondness. She ate no flesh nor anything superfluous, and when she needed food, that which she might eat appeared to be always at hand. That she might lose all relish of what she ate she was taught to carry always about her some dust of aloes, and when she found herself taking pleasure in any food or preferring one kind to another she secretly sprinkled it with a little of the bitter power before eating it. Her eyes were always cast down; she never laughed, and recognized no one who passed her, for she was so occupied with what was taking place within that her sense of exterior things was, as it were, dead.

She seemed ever discontented, yet was ever most content. She tried to rob herself of sleep by placing rough objects in her bed, but God would not permit this, for however she resisted it, sleep overcame her against her will. When Humanity saw all this spiritual ardor, and that itself was no more esteemed than if it were not, and that there was no help for it, it was greatly dissatisfied, yet, like a thief in prison who dares not utter a word in his own behalf because he knows the crime he has committed, it feared to make the matter worse, knowing that Christ, the Judge, was in anger against it. One hope it could have (and but one was possible), as when it is raining there is hope that bad weather will soon be over, and with this poor hope it waited in patience; but the Spirit in its vehemence restrained Humanity by so many bonds that it could find no relief but in sleep, and became withered, colorless, and dry like a stick; on this account the following conversation took place one day between the Spirit and Humanity:

CHAPTER XIV

Of the words that passed between the Spirit and Humanity.—Of the complaints made by Humanity against the fervor of the Spirit which she thought she could endure no longer.

Spirit. Tell me, Humanity, what think you of this mode of life?

Humanity. It seems to me, Spirit, that you have entered upon this course so vehemently that you will hardly be able to persevere in it; I hope that death, or at the least, infirmity, will not fail to follow, and that perhaps sooner than you think; and thus you will not be able to attain what you are seeking in this world, but will be obliged to go to purgatory, where you will suffer more in a moment than you would here in a whole lifetime. I shall be in the grave, and that will be far better for me than to live in this world. You will go into that fire where it will be worse with you than with me. Retrace your steps; I have no more to say.

Spirit. I hope that neither death nor infirmity will follow: at present, however, you are at the height of your misery. From this time forth you are purged of all bad humors; abstinence has been good for you; I see that your color and flesh are gone; the divine love will soon have consumed everything; I know that if I do not provide you with food you will wither away, but I will make such provision that everybody will be satisfied without calling on death or infirmity.

Such light was given to the Spirit that she perceived the least thing that might be injurious to her, and at once removed it. Humanity did all that was required of it without offering any resistance, for the spirit was so powerful that otherwise it would have fared all the worse. Finding itself in this situation and wholly without comfort, it said within itself:

Humanity. If I could have a little nourishment from spiritual things, and were able to content myself with what satisfies the Spirit, it would comfort me; otherwise I know not what to do, nor how to remain patient, thus tormented and imprisoned.

While occupied with these thoughts it chanced that the saint found herself in a church, and received communion, and there came upon her a ray of spiritual light with such force that both Soul and Body seemed to have entered together into life eternal (according to those words: Cor meum et caro mea exultaverunt, etc.). So great was the illumination and the feeling of divine things which they enjoyed that even Humanity feasted upon them, and said:

Now in this way I could live, but when that moment had passed, and this new vision had been seen by her in the light of pure love, she began to exclaim: Oh, Master, Master, I ask no sign from thee. I ask not for sensible delights, rather would I flee from them as from demons, for they are hindrances to pure love, which should be bare, lest man should with spirit and with body attach himself to it under the pretext of perfection. I pray thee, Lord, give not such things to me, they are not for me, nor for him who desires pure love in its simplicity.

CHAPTER XV

Humanity complains that the Spirit does not keep its promises and the Spirit defends itself against this charge.—Of the perils of spiritual delights under the semblance of good, and how they are more dangerous than bodily pleasures, which are evidently contrary to the Spirit.—Of the threats of the Spirit against its Humanity.

When Humanity found how hateful to the Spirit was that food upon which it fed and hoped always to feed, it was greatly dissatisfied and turned again to address her. It seemed to the body that there was no just cause why nourishment should be refused it, and especially now that it had become spiritual, for the Spirit had promised that the time would come when it too should be satisfied with the things that were according to the spirit; but, finding the contrary to be the case, and that the Spirit had no desire even for spiritual food and unwilling to regale the body with it, Humanity spoke as follows:

Humanity. You do not keep your promises, Spirit, and it will be impossible for me to persevere in such austerity without some nourishment, either natural or spiritual.

Spirit. You complain, and, as you think, with reason: I will, therefore, explain myself. You have misunderstood me. I did, indeed, promise that in the end you should be contented with what contents me, but you are looking for what will fatten, and not for what will satisfy; and not for what will satisfy; and because I am not pleased with this sensible delight, nay, even abhor it, I would have you abhor it also. You still have natural cravings for this pleasure, and you think I ought to gratify them; know that I wish to deaden and to regulate them that they may desire only in accordance with my pleasure: it is plain that you are infirm, and I shall treat you as a sick person should be treated. What you desire would injure your health; and since you affirm that spiritual delights are given by God and cannot do harm, know that your intellect partakes also of sensuality and therefore you are not a good judge; my desire is to devote myself to love, pure and simple, which attaches itself to nothing which can excite either a natural or a spiritual sentiment or feeling, and I declare to you that I dread far more an attachment to a spiritual than to a natural delight.

This is because the spiritual recaptures man under the pretext of being a good, and it is impossible without great difficulty to make him understand that it is not one; thus he continues to nourish himself on that which weans him from God. But in good truth I tell you that these hinges must of necessity be shunned by him who wishes to enjoy God as simply and purely as may be, for they are like venom to the pure love of God; and spiritual pleasure must be fled from as from the devil himself; because wherever it fastens itself it produces incurable infirmities which man does not perceive; but, believing that he is well, sees not that he is hindered from perfect good, that is, God himself, pure, simple, separated from all things human.

But natural gratifications, being evidently contrary to the spirit, cannot be disguised under the appearance of good, and I do not fear them as much. The contentment and the peace that will give you are that which will satisfy me, and which, I am certain, will also satisfy you; but it is impossible that you should yet attain it, being still far too impure.

I wish first to cleanse the house and then to adorn and fill it with good things, which will satisfy us both but nourish neither. And because you say that you cannot endure this, know that I must compel you to endure it; what cannot be done in one year can be done in ten. I am not sorry to combat with you, being willing to subdue you by any means; I wish to free myself from this constant goading at my heels, for otherwise it will never be well with me. You are gall and poison in every viand that I attempt to taste, and until I have destroyed you I shall never be at peace, for you seem bent upon doing your worst. I too shall do what is possible to free myself quickly from you; yet the worst that I can do to you will but redound to your benefit and advantage. I warn you not to get angry with me, for you can never obtain your desire and purpose in that way, but rather the contrary; console yourself with patience unmixed with hope. Conform for the present to my will—hereafter I may do yours.

CHAPTER XVI

Humanity prays the Spirit to act justly and with equity, reminding her that she had been the first to sin and that the body had been merely the instrument.—The Spirit proves the contrary, and shows who has been the cause of their fall.—The Spirit demonstrates also the necessity of purification here, and that it is better to suffer for a thousand years in this world than one hour in purgatory.

Humanity. I am, as you see, very dissatisfied and unhappy; I can escape from what you wish neither by reason nor by force; yet I implore you to satisfy me in this matter, and then you may continue what you have begun and I will have what patience I can. Oh, Spirit, you who are bringing me to justice, I pray you deal justly with me. You know that I am only a body, bestial, without reason, without prayer, without will, and without memory; because all these are in the spirit, and I work as an instrument and can do nothing but what you will. Tell me; have you not been the first to sin, with the reason and with the will? Have I been more than the instrument of sin, truly conceived and resolved upon in the spirit? Who, then, deserves the punishment?

Spirit. Your reasoning seems at the first sight to be very good; yet I believe I can refute it satisfactorily, as I intend to do.

If you, Humanity, never have sinned and never can sin, as you maintain, God, who has made the body to accompany the Soul wherever she goes, to heaven as well as to hell, must be as unjust judge; for, whoever does neither good nor evil should have neither reward nor punishment; but, since it is impossible for God to be unjust, it follows that my reasoning is sound. I confess I was the first to commit sin, for, having free-will, I cannot be constrained against it, nor can either good or evil be done if I do not first consent. If I resolve upon the good, heaven and earth yield me their support, and on every side I am encouraged to perform it; it is not possible that I should be impeded, either by the devil, or by the world, or by the flesh.

If I am bent upon evil, I find also support on every side, from the devils, the world, and myself, that is, from the flesh and its malignant instincts; and since God rewards all that is good and punishes all that is evil, it follows that all who aid in doing good will be rewarded, and all who aid in doing evil will be punished. You know that in the beginning I wished to follow my spiritual inclinations, and commenced with great impetuosity; but you assailed me with so many reasons and under the plea of such pressing necessity, that we were in continual conflict with each other; then Self-Love came as a mediator, disagreed with both, and led us so far astray that to please you and supply your needs I left the right path, and for this we shall be justly punished. It is true that if that great misery, mortal sin, is found among us, which God forbid, I, as the chief and the most noble, shall be more sorely tormented than you, but we shall both wish that we had never been created. Therefore it behooves us to purify ourselves, not alone from every stain of sin, but also from every smallest imperfection which we have contracted through our evil habits. I will tell you, moreover that God has given me a light so subtle and clear that of a surety, unless I fail before I leave you, there will remain in me no single taint of imperfection either of soul or body.

Note this well: How long, think you, will this season of purification last? You know well that it can endure but a short time. In the beginning it seems terrible to you, but as it goes on you will suffer less, because your wicked habits will be destroyed; do not fear lest you should want powerful support, for know that God, by the decree of his goodness, never allows man to suffer beyond his strength. If we regarded our own proper good, it would seem better to us to suffer here for a little than to remain in torments forever; better to suffer for a thousand years every woe possible to this body in this world, than to remain one

176

hour in purgatory. I have briefly made this little speech for your comfort.

CHAPTER XVII

God pours into and diffuses throughout the soul a divine sweetness, whereat she complains, not desiring any proof of love.—God, notwithstanding, leaves her plunged in a sea of divine love.—He gives her, also, a vision of pure Love, and another of Self-Love and of her own evil inclinations.

When the Spirit had thus satisfied Humanity, it left her and returned to its first simple and pure object, steadily pursuing that intimate and penetrating love which was so interiorly restrained that it left Humanity scarcely any breath for either natural or spiritual things, so that she seemed like one beside herself.

From the time that God established her in pure and simple love, he began to try this, his creature, with suitable temptations, mostly spiritual. He infused into her the great sweetness and divine tenderness of a most sweet love, and both Soul and Body were so overpowered by it that they could scarcely live. But as the eye of love sees all, suddenly the Soul beheld these great things, and she commenced to grieve and to say that she did not wish for such sweetness and delight in this present life, nor desire these proofs of love because they corrupt love itself.

I will guard myself, she said, as far as I am able, and neither approach them nor provide any quiet and solitary spot where I might feed upon these things, for they are poison to pure love. Yet God pursued her and kept her in the fountain of this divine sweetness; and however much the soul might protest against these proofs of his love, she nevertheless remained plunged in them as in a sea; not always in one vision, but in many and diverse.

One of these visions was that God showed her a ray of that purest love wherewith he himself loved the Soul; and the sight was such that if he had not tempered the amorous flame with a vision of Self-Love with which, the Soul saw herself stained, she could not have lived.

He showed her at another time a vision of herself, that is, of her evil inclinations, so contrary to pure love, and thus tempered that devouring flame; for after beholding it she would have rather died than offended his love in the least, not alone by sin but by imperfection. The Soul, thus occupied, neither thought nor even wished to think of her body any more than if she had none, and in this way was relieved from its annoyances, and habituated it to do her will.

CHAPTER XVIII

Humanity laments and asks for something to do.—The Spirit consents and enjoins upon it that it should be obedient to all things, stopping at nothing for any pleasure or displeasure that it might feel therein.—Of the rules he wishes to observe; and of the prohibition he imposes upon it of forming no particular friendships.

When Humanity perceived that its path became daily narrower, it again addressed the Spirit, and said humbly and with great fear and reverence:

Humanity. I find that you have deprived me of every human, external consolation, so that I may count myself as dead to the world; and if you persevere in this strictness, I see that the time will come when I shall desire death rather than lead any longer such a life.

Spirit. I am willing to give you something external to do, but it will not be agreeable. You will even abhor it, but if you complain it will be the worse for you.

Humanity. I shall be entirely satisfied if only I can have some employment.

Spirit. I warn you in the outset that I wish to teach you what it is to be obedient, in order that you may become humble, and subject to every creature; and that you may be trained to this, you shall labor for your own support. I wish, further, that whenever and wherever you are called to perform works of mercy, you should go to the infirm and to the poor of every condition. I wish you never to refuse.

You will do, as if by instinct, all that I command you, even to nursing the most loathsomely diseased persons, and whenever you are called to this duty, even should you be conversing with God, I wish you to leave all and go quickly to your work and wherever you are led; never regard either the person who summons you or the work you are to do. I wish you to have no choice; rather let the will of every other creature be yours; let your own be always thwarted.

In these exercises, so terrible to you, it is necessary to employ you, because I wish to extinguish in you every inordinate pleasure or displeasure which it is possible to feel in this life. I will root out every imperfection, and allow you to pause for either pleasure or pain no more than if you were dead. This I will see for myself, for it is necessary to try you, and therefore I shall put you to every needful proof; when I give you something abhorrent to you to do, and see that you so feel or regard it, I shall keep you at it until you do neither. I shall do likewise in those things from which you might obtain any consolation. I will force you from them until you lose all sense of pleasure or pain that might proceed therefrom. And to try you in all possible ways, you shall always be occupied in that which is either pleasurable or painful.

Moreover, you will neither form any friendship for any one, nor retain a special regard for your own kindred; but you will love every one without partiality and without affection, the poor as well as the rich, friends as well as kindred. I would wish you not really to know one from another, to make friends with no one, no matter how religious or spiritual, or to seek intimacy with none. Let it be enough for you to do your duty, as I have told you, and in this way I wish you to conduct yourself in your conversation with creatures on the earth.

CHAPTER XIX

Of the poverty in which the Spirit compelled Humanity to live.—
How she was obliged to visit the poor and sick.—Of the suffering
she found among them.—Of the oppression and interior distress
which she experienced.

After the Spirit had thus discoursed with Humanity, she found everything ordered for her in the following manner: In the first place, she was reduced to such poverty that she could not have lived, if God had not provided for her by alms.

When the Ladies of Mercy requested her, according to their custom, to visit the poor for various charitable purposes, she always went with them among these wretched beings, many of whom were intolerable from the filth and vermin with which they were covered, and some of them in their misery and want would break forth in fearful exclamations of despair, so that the entrance to their dwellings seemed like the entrance into a sepulcher, frightful to every human being. In spite of this she was eager to draw near and even touch them, that she might do something for their bodies and their souls.

There were some among the infirm who, beside their uncleanness and offensiveness, were always complaining of their attendants and loading them with abuse.

She visited, too, the poor of St Lazarus, where the greatest suffering was to be seen, as if the Spirit sent her there in search of all sorts of misery and woe. She found her task far worse than she believed, and was assailed, as it were, on both sides, namely, on the side of Humanity, which loathed these miseries, and by the Spirit, which was so lost to every external impression as to be unable to hold converse with creatures.

Humanity was so overawed by the Spirit, and thrown into such consternation by all these things, that she knew not what to do. For, on the one hand, when she was assailed by the Spirit, she would have done anything to escape its power, and when she afterwards beheld the misery of these poor creatures, she would gladly have fled from them, and yet could not. Everything was distressing to her, especially when she found that the Spirit required of her to devote herself to her work, without agitation or disgust, as she would take bread and put it into her mouth when she was hungry. And thus poor Humanity had all these difficult affairs on her hands, without a single remedy. No one could have looked upon her, in such fearful conflicts, without great compassion; but because these things were done for the attainment of liberty of spirit, everything that was required of her became easy of execution.

CHAPTER XX

Humanity having tried both exterior suffering and interior distress, the Spirit allows her to choose between them.

When the Spirit had given Humanity a trial of all the misery above described, and made her to understand all that was to be done, he thus addressed her.

Spirit. Now that you have seen for yourself what before you had only heard of, what will you do? You have tried both ways, and one of these you must pursue. You may choose for yourself, however, but with the condition, that I will make you live with creatures in a state of great subjection, as long as it shall please me; in subjection so great that you will have no place in the world where you can turn for the least repose, and I shall look to it that this shall soon begin.

Humanity. I have seen and tried the two extremes, and however great and terrible are the miseries I have witnessed, heard of, and endured, yet I would choose rather to live in the midst of them than in the piercing light of that divine ray. I fear both exterior suffering and that interior divine light which terrifies me still more; and hence I am in great perplexity.

Spirit. If you choose one of these you will not have the other; but still I warn you that you will lose everything superfluous, in order that I may live, so far as possible, pure and disengaged, as I was created; to accomplish this, I shall disregard whatever opposes me.

Humanity. Since you are so determined, all further talk would be a loss of time. I submit to all you require, and give myself up into your hands, as one dead yet still alive. Would that I were dead.

The Spirit, wishing to annihilate Humanity yet further, and finding that to approach the filth and vermin of the poor, and to touch them, overcame her with disgust, said to her: "Take some of this vermin, put it in your mouth, and eat it, if you wish to free yourself from this loathing."

When Humanity heard this, she was aghast for a moment; but she resolved at once to obey, and so doing was henceforward free.

These things were so contrary to Humanity, that no effort of nature could make them endurable; yet when she had forced herself to comply, her contentment was so great that it gave her courage for the future, and she was able to endure the outcries and complaints of impatient persons, and practice every kind of self-denial.

Thus the Spirit exercised her for about three years, all the while occupying her interior in such a manner that she performed all these acts without any interior consciousness of them, and she was made to persevere until she ceased to care for them.

CHAPTER XXI

The Spirit brings Humanity to consent to take up her abode in a hospital, where she served the sick in the humblest manner, doing everything that she was ordered to do.—When she became accustomed to whatever she naturally most abhorred, she was made directress of the hospital, and was gifted with the prudence necessary for this office.—How the burning flame of love ever increased within her.

The Spirit now obliged Humanity to take another step, requiring great submission of mind and body; namely, she was directed to live in the hospital, with her husband, and devote herself to the service of the sick; and here she was under the authority of these who governed, as if she had been their servant, hardly daring to speak, living quietly in one of the apartments, and obedient to all that was imposed upon her. When a charge was given her she fulfilled it with alacrity, although she was held in no esteem by the inmates. But of all this she had no interior recognition, for she was wholly lifted above herself, and hereupon said to the Spirit:

Humanity. If you wish me to perform these works, give me the power to do them. I refuse none of them, but they must of necessity be done with some little accidental love, or they will be ill done.

Accordingly some interest in her work was granted her, for which and with which she continued it, but it was only given just at the point where the work in which she was engaged required it, then it was taken from her, together with the memory of the work; and in these employments, and in great poverty, the Spirit left her for many years.

When the Spirit had disciplined Humanity, by such trials and humiliations, until she was able to look not only without disgust upon things which at first she naturally loathed, but busied herself unweariedly and willingly with whatever was most offensive, she was put to another trial, being placed as superior in charge of this hospital, that it might be seen if her humanity would anywhere discover itself, by reason of this elevation. She was tried by the Spirit, in this way, for many years, aided by him, however, with all needed hints and suggestions, without which she could not have fulfilled this charge. And with all these employments she remained recollected in that love which was secretly increasing as Humanity was destroyed, for just so far as she became rid of Self-Love, did she become possessed by pure love, which penetrated and filled her in proportion as she became dead to self. And thus this soul, burning with pure love, melted in that divine flame, and as this continually increased, the soul was always consuming with love; therefore she discharged all her duties with alacrity, never resting, that she might forget the flame that devoured her more and more. She never could speak of this to any one, but she talked of it to herself, unheard by others.

Now the Spirit having thus taken possession of her, said: "I will no longer call her a human creature, so entirely do I behold her in God, and with nothing human remaining."

SPIRITUAL DIALOGUES PART SECOND

Containing what God, and also the Spirit spoke to the Soul. Of the admirable ways by which God deprived her of all things and destroyed her imperfections.

CHAPTER I

Of a new love which God poured into her heart, by which he drew her Spirit to himself.—The Soul follows it, so that her powers are absorbed and lost in this love, and the Body, being subject to the Soul, becomes bewildered and changed from its natural condition.

After this creature had been despoiled of the world, of the flesh, of her possessions, habits, affections, and, in short, of everything but God, it was his will to deprive her of herself also, and to separate the Soul from the Spirit by a suffering so acute that it is difficult to describe it or to make it understood by one who has not experienced it. God infused into that heart a new love, so ardent and so powerful that it absorbed into itself the Soul, with all her powers, so that she was raised above her natural condition and so constantly occupied within herself that she could no more take delight in anything nor look toward heaven or earth.

This Soul was unable to correspond with the body, which being thrown out of its natural condition, stood bewildered, not knowing where it was, nor what to do or say. By this new method, unknown, and as yet not understood by any creature, strange and new operations were then effected. It was as if a chain were extended, by which God, who is Spirit, draws to himself the spirit of man, and holds it absorbed in him. The soul, which cannot exist without her spirit, follows, and is also thus absorbed. There she remains, unable to do otherwise, so long as God binds the spirit to himself. The body, being subject to the soul, is deprived of its natural ailment, which without her aid she cannot receive, and is thrown out of its natural state. The spirit, meanwhile, is in the fit condition for that end for which it was created by God; and, stripped of all things, it rests in him as long as it is his good pleasure, provided that the body can endure it and live.

The soul and the body then return to their natural action, and having been refreshed by the repose of the spirit, God again elevates it to its former state, and in this manner the animal imperfections are by degrees destroyed, and the soul, thus cleansed, remains pure spirit, and the body, purged from its evil habits and inclinations, is also pure and fitted to unite itself, without hindrance to the Spirit in due season. This work God effects by love alone, which is so great that it is incessantly seeking the profit and advantage of this Soul, his beloved.

But the special work of which I speak, God performs without the aid of the Soul, and in the following manner: he fills her with a secret love, which deprives her of her natural life, so that the work carried on in her is wholly supernatural. She remains meanwhile in that sea of secret love which is so great that all who are drawn within it sink overwhelmed, for it overpowers the memory, the understanding, and the will: and to these powers, thus submerged in the divine love, all things else which approached them would be their hell, for they have been deprived of the natural life for which she Soul was created.

Such a soul, while yet in this life, shares, in some degree, the happiness of the blessed; but this is hidden even from herself, for it is so great and high that she is unable to comprehend it, exceeding as it does the capacity of her powers, which look to nothing beyond, but rest satisfied and submerged in this sea of love. When created things are spoken of, her facilities, like fools, are powerless and lifeless, not knowing where they are; so hidden is this work in God. The further it advances, the more contented and strong to bear all that God pleases to accomplish in it, does the spirit become; but it comprehends no more on the account, for the soul, as if dead, knows nothing of this work nor takes any part therein.

But the body, which must needs live on this earth while God is bringing the soul by its means to her destined perfection, how can it exist, alienated in all things from its natural condition? It can no longer use the understanding, the memory, or the will, for earthly purposes, nor does it take pleasure in spiritual things. It will live, then, in this way, in great torments: but God, whose works this is, is not willing that any but himself shall take part in it, and we shall now explain the means he uses.

CHAPTER II

In what manner God keeps the Soul occupied in his love.—Of the weakness of the body and of the support it receives from creatures.—Of the extreme sufferings of Humanity, which it bemoans without complaining, being interiorly conformed to the will of God.—And how purgatory in this life is severe and sweet and full of mercy.

Sometimes this occupation of love was lightened and the Spirit allowed to take a breath, and to communicate with the Soul and the Soul with the Body, so that the senses of both were in a condition to receive some aid from created things, and were thus revived. But when God withdrew the Spirit into himself, all the rest followed it, the body remaining, as it were, dead, and so estranged from its natural state that when it again returned to it, it was entirely exhausted and could receive no help from any creature. Humanity could neither eat nor drink nor give any sign of life, so that it was led as a little child who can do nothing but weep. It could not enjoy that which nature desires, for it was deprived of taste and drawn out of its natural state.

When the Soul had remained awhile in this condition, she turned toward her Lord with bitter lamentation, and said to him:

Soul. Oh, my Lord, hitherto I have been in entire peace, contentment, and delight, for all my powers were in the enjoyment of the love bestowed on me by thee, and seemed as if they were in Paradise. Now they are driven from their home and find themselves in an unknown and strange country. Formerly the intellect, the memory, and the will, were conscious of thy love in all their operations, which they performed according to thy ordination, with great satisfaction to themselves and to all with whom they had to do: this was through thy sweet concurrence, which gave a zest to every act. Now I am naked and despoiled of all things and deprived of the power to love and to operate as I was wont to do. What then shall I do, living and yet dead, without understanding, without memory, and without will, and what is worse, without love, bereft of which I did not believe it possible to live, since man was created for love and for enjoyment, especially of God, his first object and his last end?

This operation, which I behold for the first time, deprives me of love and of joy, and I am lost in myself, not knowing what to do or say. Oh, how hard and intolerable it is to live thus, especially since I see that all my powers accord with one another, having found repose in God, their object and their end; and although they are ignorant of this work, yet in their ignorance they remain content!

But abandoned and deserted Humanity, how shall it live, parched, naked, and powerless? It has eyes and sees not; nostrils and smells not; ears and hears not; mouth and tastes not; a heart and cannot love! Every mode of life is found in that hidden love; but how is he to live to whom that love brings death, whose senses are all awake, but who cannot use them as others do?

And therefore, Humanity said, lamenting:

Me, miserable, alone in this world, what shall I do? I shall live in wretchedness, and none will have compassion on me, because this work will not be recognized as that of God, inasmuch as I must needs live, almost continually, in a different way from others, whether they be seculars or religious, and do things that will be looked upon as folly. There remains neither order nor regularity in my life, and for this reason it will rather scandalize than edify.

Alas! alas! that I should behold a work so cruel to Humanity! It is as if I were in a heated furnace, with the entrance closed, neither dead nor alive, and in dread of being reduced to ashes; yet I complain not, for interiorly I am in conformity with the will of God, who holds me in this condition according to a design neither known nor comprehended by the Soul herself; but the effect is shown in the execution of the work. It is Humanity which feels the torment, without complaining; yet if it could lament it would be refreshed.

Oh, what a sweet and cruel purgatory is this hidden one on earth! It is sweet in comparison with the purgatory of the life to come, but to us it appears cruel when we see a body on this earth suffering so intolerably. Yet what seems cruelty to us is truly a great mercy of God, although a hidden and unsuspected one. To him who is enlightened, this work is evidently done by love only the blind would endeavor to escape it, but in vain. We are all sinners, and how much better is it to be cleansed here than in the other life! For whoever suffers purgation in this life pays but a small portion of what is due, by reason of the liberty of his free-will cooperating with infused grace. God never subjects man to this discipline until he has obtained from him his free consent. For a moment it is put before him, and accepting it of his own free-will, he puts himself into the hands of God to be dealt with according to his pleasure. But this is hidden from Humanity.

The Spirit having given consent, God binds the Soul unto himself, and thereafter it remains in these bonds, which are never broken. All this is done without Humanity, which must be subject to the decree of God and the good pleasure of the Spirit. And when it finds itself in such subjection, it cries aloud like one who is suddenly wounded, and because it does not know the end, it is left to its lamentations while God continues his work, giving no heed unto its cries.

CHAPTER III

Humanity, thus menaced, desires to know the cause.—This is promised her.—God, while seeking men, draws them by different means and inspirations.—Of her continual sorrow. How, in her affliction, she calls upon God to relieve her by one ray of his love.—When she comes to understand the grace God has given her, she is pierced by a new dart of love.—Of her confession and contrition.

Humanity, finding itself menaced by various sufferings, through which it must needs pass, being unable to defend itself, sought to know the cause for which it must endure a martyrdom without alleviation. It was answered interiorly, that a release would be granted in due season, and it became as one sentenced to death, who, having heard the sentence pronounced upon his evil deeds resigns himself to an ignominious end and thus sometimes escapes it.

"In my infinite and ever-active love," spake God, "I continually go forth in search of souls, in order to guide them to life eternal; and, illuminating them with my light, I move the free-will of men in many and diverse ways. When man yields to my inspirations, I increase this light, and by its aid he sees himself imprisoned, as it were, in a foul and dismal den, surrounded by a brood of venomous reptiles which strive to destroy him but which he saw not before by reason of the darkness. By the light I grant him, he sees his peril and calls upon me to free him in mercy from the miseries which hem him in on every side. I am ever illuminating him more and more, and, as his light grows clearer, and he discovers more plainly the dangers which surround him, he cries aloud and with bitter tears: 'O my God! take me hence and do with me what thou wilt. I can endure all things if thou wilt release me from this misery and peril!'"

It appeared to this Soul that God turned a deaf ear to her lamentations; but he increased her light daily, and with its growth her anguish likewise deepened, for by it she saw not only her own danger, but that no way of escape was open to her. Long did she cry to God for help, for so he had decreed, and though he gave her no reply, he yet had regard to her perseverance, and kindled in her heart a hidden fire, while at the same time he revealed to her her imperfections. In this manner she was for a season restrained and overwhelmed in her own wretchedness. She ate no other bread, and lived in continual sorrow; moreover, as the light of grace increased, the flesh was consumed away and the blood cleansed from its superfluous humors. She was so weakened and afflicted that she could scarcely move, and in her desolation she cried aloud to God: Miserere mei Deus secundum magnam misericordiam tuam (Psalm 50).

And God, when he saw her entirely abandoned to his mercy and despairing of herself, revived her with a ray of his love whereby he made her see anew the magnitude of her defects, and that hell alone was their fitting retribution. She recognized, moreover, the singular grace which God had bestowed upon her, and as she beheld it, she was pierced afresh with love and grief at her offences against such great goodness. She began to confess her sins with such deep and extraordinary contrition that she seemed ready to perform every possible penance of soul and body.

Contrition, confession, and satisfaction, are the first works of the Soul after it has been enlightened by God. By this means she is freed from her sins and imperfections, clothed with virtue, and remains thus until she has formed the habit of virtue.

CHAPTER IV

God sends into that heart another ray of love, which, diffusing itself, fills the soul and revives the body.—There is nothing but exceeding love and joy, until this love, which is wholly from God, has completed its work.

God once more infused into the Soul another ray of love, and by its superabundance the body also was refreshed, and there was nothing but love and rejoicing of heart, for the Soul believed herself in paradise. In this state the Soul continued until every love except that of God was entirely consumed, and with his love alone she remained until she was wholly absorbed in him. He bestowed upon her many graces and sent her many sweet consolations, upon which she fed as do all those who share the divine love. He spoke to her also in those loving words which, like flame, penetrate the hearts of those who hear them. The body, moreover, was so inflamed, that it seemed as if the Soul must quit it in order to unite herself with her Love. This was to her a season of great peace and consolation, for all her nourishment was the food of eternal life.

In this state she feared neither martyrdom nor hell nor any opposition or adversity that might befall her, for it seemed to her that with this love she could endure all things. O loving and rejoicing heart! O happy soul that has tasted this love! Thou canst no longer enjoy or behold aught beside, for thou hast attained thy rest for which thou wert created! O sweet and secret love: whoever tastes thee can no longer exist without thee! Thou, O man! who wert created for this love, how canst thou be satisfied and at peace without it? How canst thou live? In it is comprised all that can be desired, and it yields a satisfaction so entire that man can neither obtain it for himself nor even conceive it until he has experienced it. O love! in which are united all bliss and all delight, and which satisfies all desire!

Whoever could express the emotions of a heart enamored of God, would break every other heart with longing, although it were harder than the diamond and perverser than the devil. O flame of love! thou dost consume all rust, and so completely removest every shadow of defect that the least imperfection disappears before thee. So perfectly dost thou thy work in the Soul, that she is cleansed even from those defects that are seen by thine eye alone, to which even that which seems to us perfection is full of faults.

O Love! thou dost wholly cleanse and purify us; thou dost enlighten and strengthen our understanding, and dost even perform for us our necessary works, and this through thy pure love alone which meets with no return from us.

And now this Soul, filled with astonishment at beholding God so enamored of her, questions him concerning his love.

CHAPTER V

The Soul asks concerning this love.—Our Lord in part answers her and discourses to her upon its greatness, nature, properties, causes and effects.

Soul. O Lord! what is that soul which thou holdest in such esteem and which we value so little? I would that I knew the cause of thy great and pure love for the rational creature whom I behold so contrary in all things to thee!

Our Lord listened favorably to her request and thus replied: "If you were to know how much I love the soul, you would never know aught further, for you would either die or continue to live by a miracle. And if you were able to compare your own misery with that great love and goodness which I never cease to exercise toward man, you would live in despair. So powerful is my love that the knowledge of it would annihilate not only the body but the soul of man, if that were possible. My love is infinite, and I cannot but love that which I have created; my love is pure, simple, and sincere, neither can I love except with such a love.

"To him who could in the least understand this, every other love would seem, what in truth it is, an aberration. The cause of my love is only love itself; and because you cannot comprehend, it be at peace and seek not for what you cannot find. This, my love, is better comprehended by an interior sense than by any other way, and to acquire this the action of love must wholly detach man from himself, for he is his own worst impediment. This love destroys malice and fits man to understand the nature of love."

O admirable work of love, which gives God to man that he may do all that is needful to attain that perfection for which he is designed! God gives him, too, all needful light and grace, increasing them gradually in such a manner and to such a degree that they never fail and never exceed; for if they fell short, man might excuse himself from doing his part because grace was wanting to him, and if they exceeded, the work he might have done through their means but failed to do, would be his punishment.

Grace increases in proportion as man makes use of it. Hence it is evident that God gives man from day to day all that he needs, no more and no less, and to each according to his condition and capacity. All this he does for the love and benefit of man; but because we are so cold and negligent in our endeavors, and because the instinct of the spirit is to arrive quickly at perfection, it seems as if grace were insufficient. Yet it is not so, and the fault is wholly ours, in not cooperating with the grace already received, which therefore ceases to increase.

O wretched man! how shall you be excused for failing to correspond with that great love and care which God has always bestowed and still bestows upon you? At the hour of death you will behold and know all this, and you will then be speechless through astonishment. Then the truth will be made plain and you will have no power to contradict it. Shame will overpower you for having failed to do your part in response to all this aid, this grace, this loving care of your Lord, who, in order to satisfy your other request, speaks to you thus:

CHAPTER VI

God reveals to the Soul that the body is to be purgatory for her in this world.—How necessary it is that man should deny himself and become wholly lost in God.—Of the misery of man when he occupies himself with aught beside, since he has no time but the present to acquire a treasure of merit.

The Lord. The cause of all the suffering through which you have to pass is better understood by experience than by reasoning. Yet know this: I make of the body a purgatory for the soul, and thus augment her glory by drawing her to me through this purgatory alone. And thus I am ever knocking at the door of the heart, and if man yields consent and opens to me, I lead him with continual and loving care to that degree of glory for which I created him. If he could see and understand the care with which I promote his salvation and his welfare, quitting and despising all ease, even were the universe at his command, he would abandon himself without reserve to me.

There is no martyrdom that he would not endure, if it would preserve him from losing this loving care which is leading him to the highest glory. I would draw him to me by love and faith alone, to which fear and self-interest are opposed, because they spring from the love of self, which cannot coexist with that pure and simple love which alone must absorb man if he would not cast off my care of him. Without this aid he could not enter into the clear depths of my love, for it would be a hell to him. And man, having no other way and no other time but this life in which to purify his soul by love and faith, and with the assistance of my grace, is it not a misery for him to occupy himself with aught beside, and thus lose the precious time which was given him for this work alone? Once passed, it will never more return. Listen then, O Soul, my beloved! listen to my voice; open thine ears to thy Lord who so much loves thee, who is ever caring for thee, and who alone is thy salvation! Steeped in sin as thou art, sunk in such misery and weighed down with evil habits, thou wilt never know the greatness of thy woes until my light unveils them to thee and frees thee from them!

Soul. Thou hast given me, Lord, many persuasive reasons why I should suffer as I have done and must still do; yet, I pray thee, if it please thee, satisfy my understanding concerning the cause of this suffering, for I need it greatly when I am overpowered by the vehemence of thy love.

The Lord. Thou knowest that when thou didst yield up thy will to me thou wert sunk so low that had I not prevented thee thou wouldst have fallen into hell. Thou wert borne away into sin and misery like one bound hand and foot. I granted thee light and contrition, by the help of which thou didst make thy confession. Thou hast performed many penances, and for a long time offered prayers and alms in satisfaction for thy sins. I left thee to struggle and torment thyself until thou wert well established in virtue, that thou mightest not hence forward fall into sin. I allowed thee to practice various virtues in order that thou shouldst be confirmed and take pleasure in them and never more turn to other enjoyments.

And now the Soul began to delight in spiritual things, and was assailed by many temptations, and was thus practiced in the ways of God. The providence of God was also made plain to her in many trials and persecutions which she endured from men, from devils, and from herself. For, being accustomed to wrong-doing, it was necessary for her to combat all these enemies until she had destroyed them, inasmuch as it is they who were ever warring against her. And if it were not for our evil habits no one would ever be tempted except in consequence of the increase of grace, and this is a temptation which is without danger, because God sustains by his love those upon whom he permits it to fall.

CHAPTER VII

The Soul, confirmed in virtue, begins to rest in her Lord.—God permits her to see that loving operations whereby, through his great goodness alone, he had liberated her.—The Soul, perceiving her own miseries, burns with a continual flame and is unable to speak or thing of aught besides.

When God had despoiled this Soul of her evil habits and clothed her with virtue, and had well instructed her in the spiritual life, she began to rest in her Lord. Her battle and her servitude being ended, she was filled with a great joy, especially when God opened her eyes to see how greatly he had assisted her, and how he had defended her from her enemies, both visible and invisible, and from herself, who was the worst of all. The Soul, discerning the providence of God, and finding herself entirely freed from her interior trials, began to turn towards her Lord, who, designing to raise her to a higher state, caused her to behold with the eye of divine love the loving operation which he had accomplished in her. When she beheld his great and watchful care she was lost in astonishment, and considered what God was and what she herself was; that is, how low she was in misery and sorrow and how his goodness alone had rescued her by pure and simple love, and prepared her by amorous modes and ways to receive his divine love. This vision made her confess with bitter tears her woes and sins; and the love which God manifested to her continued to inflame her in such a manner that she could speak and think of nothing else. And in this state she remained until all other loves, both spiritual and natural, were entirely consumed.

And because the love of God, inasmuch as it is lonely and remote from other loves, is so much the greater, and more vehemently occupies the soul (for it is ever increasing, and works secretly, not only on others but also on itself), therefore the Soul, finding herself in this state, enjoyed all things, interior as well as exterior, in peace, in love, and in delight; for she did not yet know the way by which God intended to lead her, although she was approaching it. And God spake thus to her:

CHAPTER VIII

*Our Lord makes known to the Soul that she had merited nothing,
having employed in purifying herself the time which was given
her to increase in grace and glory.—Also he shows her that
without his help she could have done nothing.*

The Lord. My daughter, hitherto you have followed the odor
of my perfumes, which have guided and supported you thus far
upon your way; but without me you could have done nothing. In
this way, my grace assisting, you are purged from your sins,
despoiled of your affections, habited in virtue, burning with
love, and as it were, united with me in love, and so full of
delight, both inwardly and outwardly, that you seem to yourself
to be in paradise.

But understand that hitherto you have merited nothing, for
whatever you have done in the way of penance, fasting, alms,
and prayers, you were obliged to do; it was needful for you to
perform them all by my light in order to cancel your debts. And
having not the means wherewith to satisfy, I have granted you
these through love for you, that you might by them make
satisfaction: and know, that all this time which you have spent in
satisfying for your sins is as if it were lost, for it was given you
that you might increase in love, grace, and glory; therefore, you
have merited nothing, although it may seem to you that you have
done great things, and such as are highly esteemed by those who
do not understand them.

It was also necessary that you should be clothed with the
virtues which attract love, that they might protect you from evil
and prepare you to receive greater light; and knowing that of
yourself you were unfit for any good work and also incapable of
it, I have given you (in order that you might work and persevere

in work) a hidden love, by whose operations all your facilities and also your bodily senses should be voluntarily disposed to make satisfaction. I have given you, moreover, the power to love me, in order to detach you from every other love, and finally I have conducted you to the portals of my true and perfect love, beyond which you have not advanced, for to do so is beyond your strength. And with all this you are not yet content, for you have the instinct to advance, although you know not even what you desire.

CHAPTER IX

The Spirit, seeing the Soul brought to the gates of divine love, resolves to subject both Soul and Body to severe suffering.—He tells the Soul that he will separate himself from her, and that in order to recover her first purity, she must pass through many trials.

When the Spirit saw the Soul led to the portals of divine love, from which she was neither able to advance nor to recede, and saw, moreover, that she had been conducted thus far with much assistance from God, who had pleasantly occupied without wholly satisfying all her facilities, he thus spake:

Spirit. Now is the time for me to repay the Soul for what she has done to me. For many years I have been subject to her, and, with cruelties too great to be described, excluded from my home; for she was so restrained and oppressed by earthly things that the powers I possessed were not sufficient to enable me to attend to my own spiritual concerns. I called to my aid the certainty of death, the fear of hell, the hope of heaven, preaching, and all other aids afforded by the Church; and also divine inspirations, infirmities, poverty, and other worldly tribulations, in order that, deprived of all things earthly, she might, in her extreme need, when all other resources had failed her, have recourse unto God. But, though in her great necessity she sometimes turned to him and promised with his assistance to do great things, yet when that moment was passed she returned to her accustomed practices and I to my prison; and this has happened many times. But now that I see my Soul, with her senses, and also those of the body, arrived at a point from which she can neither advance nor recede, I will subject and restrain them all in such a way that they can neither impede nor retard me. Complaints will not avail them; they will be as much at my discretion as I have been at theirs; but I shall not be as cruel to them as they have been to me, for they never afforded me the smallest help, even when I was most oppressed and surrounded by my enemies. I will keep the Soul in restraint and in subjection, and inflict upon her, without mercy, all the suffering she can bear. I have her in my hands, and I will leave her so naked, desolate, and forsaken, that she will know not where to turn except for the bare necessities which will keep her alive to suffer a yet longer martyrdom; and this will be in secret in order that no one may give her any remedy. Not one of her members shall escape suffering until my work is finished; whosoever shall behold her in such torments will wish her dead, and she would herself wish it if she could do so without sin.

Soul. I have heard enough of your threats, and am sufficiently well acquainted with the prospect of what I am to suffer; but the reason of this suffering I have not been able to understand, although it has been promised to me.

Spirit. I mean to separate myself from you, and for the present I will answer you in words; hereafter I will do so more effectually by deeds which will make you envy the dead.

You have been conducted even to this threshold by many gentle means and divine graces, which you have assumed and appropriated to yourself, and have hidden them with a subtlety of which you are not yourself aware, for they have become your by such long use that no eye but that of God can discern them; neither would you believe it, did not God himself declare it. Gradually you will come to understand by experience, that even in the first light that was given you, you appropriated your share, and so of contrition, confession, satisfaction, prayer, and other virtuous acts; of interior and exterior detachment; of the sweet love of God, of the alienation of the bodily senses, so that they appeared as if dead because they were entirely controlled by the divine operation. And inasmuch as those works had long sustained your faculties, and the love of God was so strong and powerful within you, you seemed to yourself to be in heaven, and enjoyed it all within yourself as if it were yours by right, and had been bestowed on you by God as the reward of your merits. You did not return it wholly and entirely to him as you should have done in all simplicity and uprightness, and in this you have been dishonest and have defiled yourself, and therefore you must suffer all I have foretold you. Learn what a task it is to purge a soul here below and restore her with no further purgatory to her pristine purity. And when it is God's will to elevate her to a high degree of glory, it becomes more especially necessary, not alone to purify her but to make her pass through many cruel sufferings that she may gain merit by many and grievous pains.

When the time came which pleased God, he drew the Spirit so secretly and closely to himself, that it held no communication with the Soul nor the Soul with the Body, and both were left so bare and dry that it was hard for them to live at all, and especially at the first, when they were passing from one extreme to the other, although God was secretly attracting them by little and little. At length that befell the Soul, which happens to a bombshell, when the fire being applied it explodes and loses both fire and powder; thus the Soul, having conceived the fire of pure, divine love, suddenly lost that which had before inflamed her, and, deprived of all sensibility, could never more return to it. She resembled a musical instrument which, while furnished with strings, sends forth sweet melody, but, being deprived of them, is silent. So she, who had hitherto with the senses of both Soul and body, discoursed such sweet music, now, bereft of these, remained stringless and mute. When she found herself closely pressed by the Spirit, with no hope of relief (for she remembered all his threats), she cried to God, and said:

CHAPTER X

The Soul discovers that she must make satisfaction voluntarily, and it seems to her that she is abandoned by God.—She calls upon others for help.—How Humanity, by whom she had been threatened, is put to the proof.—Of the sufferings of the Body when deprived of communications with the Spirit.

Soul. Lord, I see it to be necessary that I should atone for my dishonest appropriation of thy spiritual graces, and I begin to understand that as I have consented to take part with the body in sin, and have found pleasure in it, I must also consent that it shall be expiated by my own sufferings as well as by those of the body, and that I must pay, even to the last farthing. I see that I have secretly robbed thee of what was thine, and have appropriated many satisfactions, and delighted in many spiritual graces, without referring them all to thee as was my duty; namely, many sweet consolations in speaking, hearing, tasting, and in various other things. I perceive that this robbery was very serious, since nothing more precious could be stolen. For these are the things which essentially differ from all that is man's own. Nothing is of real value to him, except that which it pleases thee to give him by thy grace. Therefore it is necessary for us to comprehend that every grace proceeds from thee, and to thee it must be returned, if we would not be robbers: this robbery originated with the devil by whom we are continually tempted and by whom many are led astray.

But how shall I satisfy myself for this great and subtle sin, since I have neither strength nor feeling, either of soul or body? I know not whether I am alive or dead. It is hard to live in this world, and yet I must both live and suffer greatly, in order to expiate my offences. I seem to be abandoned by the divine and through the knowledge of that which, not to others but to thee alone, my God, is fully known, that I would always rob thee. Finding myself deserted on every side, give me at least one who can understand and comfort me, as is done to the condemned, that they may not wholly despair.

Then God comforted Humanity somewhat, and afterwards exercised her in that with which she had before been threatened. The body by degrees became infirm, being deprived of the correspondence of the Spirit, which held the powers of the Soul suspended and engaged, while the body remained naked, famished, wretched, and unconscious that this was the work of God. Hence, it rapidly consumed away and felt every slight evil as a great calamity, and its infirmity increased to such a degree that if it kept the Soul intent on some hidden operation, the body would not have been able to support itself. Exteriorly, too, he gave her a director adapted to her need, who comprehended the work of God within her. This was a great consolation, for her natural forces could not have sustained her under trials so great that they could neither be described by human tongue, nor, if described, be understood. Even if witnessed by the bodily eye they would be incomprehensible, so much greater was the interior suffering than the exterior, and so impossible was it for any way or kind of relief to be found. But God now and then afforded Humanity a little relief, and she seemed restored, although the interior oppression was constantly increasing. So she wandered about the house, wasting away, and ignorant of the nature of her malady, so subtle, hidden, and penetrating was that divine work.

Then she was assailed in a different manner and with strange and new afflictions, against which she struggled with all her powers. When God afflicted the body, he fortified the mind, and when the mind was suffering, he consoled the body, and thus supported each in turn. She continued in this state for about ten years, Humanity being always more and more unconscious of those hidden operations by which God held her, as it were, bound.

211

Afterwards he took from her her confessor, and everything else towards which she looked for help. Then the Spirit drew her forcibly to himself, because he, in turn, was drawn by God with a hidden love, so penetrating and powerful, though without delight, that it melted into itself both Soul and Spirit, while the bodily senses, with everything else, were absorbed in God.

This hidden love checked, purged, and exterminated all those sins of robbery which had been so secretly and cunningly committed, and thus in secret the penance was performed while the cause remained concealed. Humanity was so oppressed and crushed that she was constrained to cry to our Lord in piteous accents:

"Oh, my God! how hast thou abandoned me to such cruel sufferings, both interior and exterior! Yet, while I suffer I am still unable to complain, for even when I am most grievously afflicted, I am in secret satisfied by a sharp and searching flame of love, which is gradually consuming all my natural and spiritual strength, so that it is most strange to see a creature living thus deprived of vital force. My confessor, too, is taken from me, so that I can no longer take counsel of him, and so weak have I become that I can turn to nothing with any spirit. Interiorly I find the secret strength which was given me decaying, nor am I in a condition to receive anything from heaven, or earth, but am left like one dead. Yet I must live so long as it pleases God, though I know not how I can live without the help which I am not even able to receive when it is offered me."

CHAPTER XI

Of the brightness of eternal glory, and of the strength imparted to Humanity by a glimpse of it.—How God draws the Spirit to himself, so that it may be wholly occupied in him.—Of its sufferings.—What it is to live on earth while the Spirit is in heaven, and through what sufferings one must pass in order to escape purgatory.

Towards the close of this process, God came to her aid in a different manner. He sometimes revealed to her a ray of that glory towards which she approached, as the affections of the Soul and the bodily sensations became weaker. This revived her so much, both interiorly and exteriorly, that it supported her for many days; for although she beheld it but a moment, the impression, without any renewal, remained within. And she saw that God held her Spirit so fixed upon himself that he did not allow it to weaver for an instant. The longer this continued the more difficult it was to withdraw from it, the difficulty being too great for words to express. And this was by reason of that hidden Spirit which found itself drawn into greater depths the higher it ascended towards God, and continually losing its own strength as it became more and more absorbed in God, who thus spake to the Soul:

The Lord. Henceforth I will not have you interfere with my designs, for you would always rob me by appropriating to yourself what is not yours. I will finish the work, and you shall be unconscious of it. I will separate you from your Spirit, and he shall be lost in my abyss.

Humanity on hearing this was filled with consternation, and said:

"I am in misery. I do not live, and yet I cannot die, but find myself every day more and more oppressed, and, as it were, consuming away. When I beheld what it was to be centered entirely in God without a single moment's respite, and that I was myself the miserable creature who was to support this siege, and how very terrible it was, all my flesh was in torment. To remain thus steadily occupied in God, without a moment's wavering, is a thing for the blessed in heaven, who, lost to themselves, live only in him. That I should live in this way upon earth while my Spirit is in heaven, is a work surpassing all that I have known, and is the most terrible suffering that can be endured in this world."

It was shown to Humanity that whoever would enter life eternal without passing through purgatory, must die to this world while yet in it; that is, that all the imperfections of the Soul must be so consumed that she may remain absorbed in God. "But hearing thee weep, O Humanity! it is plain that thou art not yet dead, and thou must still live until thou findest life without impediment. When thy vivacity is all passed away, and thy sensibility is weakened, thou wilt have less to endure. Thou wilt not anticipate thy sufferings afar off as now thou dost, with agitation, but wilt abandon thyself to God, not through the powers of the Soul, nor through any instinct of nature, but purely because God has taken upon himself all these things, and works so secretly and subtly that he in whom the work is wrought is not himself aware of it."

This God does, that man may be sensible of the suffering inflicted on him, for otherwise he would feel it less, and if he comprehended what was going on, he would always be guilty of robbery, even if he were not led to it by his evil instincts, united to the bad habits, hidden in the depths of his soul. But God, knowing that man could not live in so great an extremity if he did not provide for him, does so secretly and in various modes and times, according to his necessity. At first the assistance is very evident, that he may with love persevere and form the habit of doing spiritual works; then, by degrees, God withdraws these supports whenever he finds the man strong enough to endure the battle. The greater strength he has at the beginning, the greater suffering he may look for toward the end, although God always assists him according to his necessities; yet he does this far more secretly than openly, and never ceases but at death.

SPIRITUAL DIALOGUES PART THIRD

Containing some questions concerning the love of God towards man, proposed by the Soul to her Lord, and his loving answers, the truth of which was afterwards entirely proved by the Blessed One herself.

CHAPTER I

The Soul inquires of God the reason of his great love for man, who is so opposed to him; and also what is man, for whom he cares so much.

Soul. O, Lord, when I see thee so enamored of man, I long to know the cause of this great love, especially as in his manner of life, man is so opposed to thy will, estranged from thy love, averse to thy operations, contrary to thee in all things, full of this world, blind, deaf, dumb, and stupid, without the power and without the means of acting according to thy will. I confess, O Lord, that I know not what is this man of whom thou art so mindful; I know not whether thou art his master or his servant; it seems to me as if love had so blinded thee that thou seest not the depth of his miseries. I pray thee, O my Lord, to satisfy me fully in this matter.

The Lord. You demand a thing beyond your comprehension; yet, in order to satisfy your understanding, which in these matters is weak and uninformed, I will show you a scintillation of this love which if you should behold clearly you could not live if I did not sustain you by my grace.

Know then, in the first place, that I am God, with whom there is no change; and know too that I loved man before I created him. I loved him with a love which is infinite, pure, simple, and sincere, and without any cause; it is impossible that I should not love those whom I have created and designed for my glory, each in his own degree. I have also provided him amply with all needful means of attaining his end, both with natural gifts and supernatural graces, and on my part these never fail him. I am ever surrounding him with my infinite love, now in one way and now in another, that I may bring him under my care. I find in him nothing which is contrary to me but the free-will which I have given him, and this I am always combating through love, until he yields it to me, and when I have accepted it I reform it little by little by my secret operations and loving care, and never abandon him until I have conducted him to his appointed end.

To your other question, as to why I love man, who is opposed to me and laden with sins that are so hateful in the sight of heaven, I answer, that by reason of the infinite bounty and pure love with which I love him, I can neither see his defects nor fail to accomplish my work, which is purely to benefit him; I cast such a light on his defects that perforce he sees them, and doing so he bewails them, and bewailing them he purges himself from them. He offends me only when he puts hindrances in the way by which I am endeavoring to lead him to his end; that is, when he hinders me, by mortal sin, from accomplishing my loving designs according to his necessities. But that love which you desire to know is beyond your comprehension, for it has neither form nor limit; neither can you know it through the intellect, for it is not intelligible; it is in part made known by its effects, which are small or great in proportion to the measure of love which is brought into action.

If one who had not lost faith should desire to see the effects of this work which is accomplished in man by that spark of love which infuses into his heart, be assured that he would be so inflamed by love that he could not live, for so great would be its power that he would melt away and be no more. Though men are for the most part forever in ignorance of it, yet, for this hidden love, you see those who abandon the world, leave their possessions, friends, and kindred, and hold in abhorrence all other loves and joys. For this love men have sold themselves as slaves, and remained in bondage to others until death; and its force increases so continually that they would suffer martyrdom for it a thousand times, as they have often done and will ever continue to do.

You see this love transforms beasts into men, men into angels, and angels becoming God, as it were, by participation. You see men changed from earthly into heavenly, and devoting themselves with both soul and body to the practice of spiritual things. Their whole life and manner of speech are altered, and they do and say the contrary of what was formerly their custom. All are surprised at this, and yet it seems good to all, and men are almost envious of it.

But unless by experience, no one comprehends how this has been brought about. That deep sweet, and penetrating love which man feels in his heart is unknown, and can neither be described nor understood except by the light of the affections in whose exercise he feels himself occupied, bound, transformed, in peace and harmony with the bodily sensations, and without any contradiction, so that he has nothing, wills nothing, and desires nothing. He remains quiet and satisfied in his inmost heart, knowing this love and knowing it alone. He is kept closely bound by a very subtle thread, held secretly by the hand of God, who leaves him to struggle and combat with the world, the devils, and himself, while fainting weak, and helpless, he fears ruin on every side but God does not let him fall.

The true love which you are striving, O Soul, to comprehend, is not this, but is seen only when I have consumed the imperfections of man by every mode of human misery, both exterior and interior. As for that which cannot be seen, this is my mode of action. I let down into the heart of man the slender, golden thread of my hidden love, to which is attached a hook which enters the heart, and man feels himself wounded, but knows not by whom he is bound and taken. He neither moves nor wishes to move, because his heart is drawn by me, its object and its end, although he does not comprehend it; but it is I who hold the thread in my hand, and draw it even closer with a love so penetrating and so subtle, that man is conquered and subdued and entirely taken out of himself.

As the feet of one who has been hanged do not touch the earth, but his body remains attached to the cord by which he received his death, so the Spirit remains suspended by the slender thread of love whereby all the subtle and hidden imperfections of man receive their death: all that he now loves he loves by virtue of the tie by which he is bound. All his actions are done by means of that love and through sanctifying grace, because it is now God who works alone, by his pure love and without man's assistance. And God, having thus taken man into his own keeping, and drawn him entirely to himself, so enriches him with his favors that when he comes to die he finds himself drawn unconsciously by that thread of love into the divine abyss. And although man in this state appears a lifeless, lost, and abject thing, yet his life is hidden in God amid the treasures of eternal life; nor can it be told or imagined what God has prepared for this beloved Soul.

The Soul, hearing all this, is so inflamed by ardent love that she breaks forth into exclamations:

CHAPTER II

Exclamations of the Soul.—Our Lord demands the cause of her surprise, and questions her concerning her enjoyment in the company of spiritual persons, and of the pleasing conversations held with them.

Soul. O tongue, why dost thou speak, when thou canst find no fitting words for the love felt by my heart? O heart, inflamed with love, why dost thou not consume the body where thou dwellest? O Spirit, what dost thou, thus bound upon the earth? Seest thou not that vehemence of love wherewith God attracts and desires thee? Destroy this body, that each may go to his own place!

And God, when he beheld the Soul kindled with a flame so great and limitless, desiring in some measure to restrain her, showed her one spark of that love with which he loves man, and which is so pure, simple, and sincere that the Soul when she beheld it was wellnigh overpowered with astonishment; then the Lord demanded of her, saying:

The Lord. Why do I behold you thus changed? What new thing have you seen that kindles in you such a flame of love? Hitherto you have seemed ready to break through the body in order to find your love, by reason of the great delight and sweet enjoyment you tasted, together with many other of your friends, with whom you were united in the bonds of that sweet and winning love; but now I see you pausing and bewildered, and caring to converse with no one.

Until now this Soul had often occupied herself in conversing with her spiritual friends on the divine love, until it seemed to them as if they were already in paradise. Oh, how sweet were these colloquies! Both he who spoke and he who listened were fed alike upon that spiritual, sweet, and delicious food, and were not satisfied to see time pass so quickly while they talked, but all inflamed and burning, could neither speak nor separate, and seemed as if beside themselves. O feasts of love! O food most exquisite! What delicious viands, what sweet union, what divine company! They spoke only of the love of God, of its operations, and how all hindrances to it might be removed. All that took place between them was so clearly seen to be from God and for the benefit of souls, that no one could think otherwise, and hence the Soul responded:

CHAPTER III

*The Soul discovers that what she had been doing, as if for God,
proceeded truly from Self-Love.—She is filled with astonishment
at the sight of pure love, and inquires concerning its nature.—
Our Lord answers her that she could not understand it, and that
he himself, being love, can be comprehended only in his effects.*

Soul. Thou hast shown me, O Lord, another light in which I
have seen that it is Self-Love which has hitherto moved me, and
that all which has had the semblance of being wrought so
lovingly for thee and in thee was self-defiled and of my own
doing, and secretly appropriated to myself. It was hidden in me,
my God, beneath thy shadow, under which I rested. But now that
I behold thy simple, pure, and ardent love, with its operations, I
am lost and bewildered, and all other loves seem to me worse
than selfish. O divine love, where shall I find words to speak of
thee? I am conquered and subdued by thee; I am dying of love
and I do not feel love; I am annihilated in love and I do not know
love; I feel love acting within me, and its action I do not
understand; I feel my heart burning with love, and yet I do not
see the flame of love.

O my God, I cannot cease to search for tokens of thy care;
and although I am wholly overpowered by the new light which
thou hast shown me, I do not yet despair of knowing more fully
this love which, containing within itself everything that is
desirable in heaven and on earth, satisfies man without satiating
him, and even constantly increases the appetite which feeds
upon it. It is so sweet and gentle, this pure and simple love, and
so adapted to the heart of man, that he who has once enjoyed it,
though but a little, would never cease to seek it, though the
search should cost him a thousand lives. What is this love which

conquers all things? Thou, Lord, hast told me many things concerning it, but they all seem to me to fall short; and since thou hast given me the burning desire to penetrate it more deeply, I will not believe that it can be in vain. Thou hast promised me a fuller satisfaction than I have attained. Thou hast shown me a spark of thy pure and simple love, and it has kindled in my heart a flame that devours me. Nowhere on earth can I find repose, nor can I feel or see aught beside. I am lost and beside myself; I am led captive and wounded nigh unto death, and wait only on thy providence, which will satisfy every one of my desires, which is in the order of salvation.

The Lord. O Soul, my beloved, thou art seeking to know what thou canst not comprehend. Thy instinct and thy desire, so far as the natural man is concerned, are supernatural; but as concerning the spiritual, and the end for which thou wert created, they are natural, because love is thy beginning, thy middle, and ought to be thy end. Thou canst not live without love, for it is thy life, both in this world and in the other. It is for this reason that the desire consumed thee to know what love may be, but thou canst not comprehend it with the intellect, nor with the Spirit, nor with all the love thou mayest possess; even those who are in heaven, their home, know it only according to the measure of grace and charity they have had in this life.

For love is God himself, who cannot be comprehended, except by the wonderful effects of the great love which he is ever manifesting, and which can neither be estimated nor imagined. And when I reveal to the Soul but one spark of my pure love, she is constrained to return me that love, whose power compels her to do her all for me, even, if need were, to suffer torture and a thousand deaths. How much love may be infused into the hearts of men, can be learned from what men have done for love of me. But I see, my beloved, that thou seekest not this operative love in its effects, but those gentle drops that I pour into the hearts of my elect, and which melt the Soul, the Spirit, and even the bodily powers, so that they act no longer. By these drops the Soul remains immersed in the sweetness of that love, and is incapable of performing any action: she is lost in herself and alienated from every creature: serene in the depths of her heart, at peace with all, and passive, she is absorbed with that love, which satisfies her, without nourishment; hence she exclaims in her ardor:

Soul. O food without taste, O taste without flavor, O flavor without food, O food of love on which angels, saints, and men are nourished! O beatific food, he who tastes thee knows not what thou art! O real food, satisfying the appetite, thou dost destroy every other desire! He who enjoys this food esteems himself already blessed even in this life, where God communicates it but in the smallest measure: if he should bestow only a little more, man would die of that subtle, penetrating love, for the Spirit would be so inflamed that the weak body would perish. O celestial love! O divine love! thou hast sealed my lips: I know not how to speak, nor will I seek what never can be found. I am conquered and overpowered.

CHAPTER IV

That he whose heart is pure knows the love of God.—How that love works secretly, subtly, and without exterior occupation.— Some of its effects.—Exclamations of the Soul upon this love.— Of its properties.

The Lord. O beloved Soul, knowest thou who it is that employs my love? He whose heart is pure and empty of every other love. When he has found it, he remains content and satisfied, although he knows not my mode of operation nor his own condition; because love works in secret and subtly, without external show.

Such a one is continually occupied, yet without occupation; he is bound, yet knows not who holds him, he is in a prison without an outlet. The Soul can avail herself of neither her understanding, her memory, nor her will, and seems like a thing insensate, dumb, and blind, because the divine love has overpowered all the sensibilities of both Soul and Body. And therefore the Soul and Spirit, finding themselves so transformed from their wonted habit of loving and acting, and secretly and strongly swayed by a higher love, are constrained to ask: "O Lord, what manner of love is this? What is this love which is ever changing man from good to better, continually bringing him nearer to his end, and yet, as he approaches it more closely, plunges him into ever profounder ignorance of his situation?"

Man in this state is kept alive by the rays of love with which God pierces his heart, and which return to heaven in ardent sighs. If he did not find this relief he would die through the vehemence of this fire. Sometimes it so restrains him that he can neither speak nor sigh, in order that its work may be more quickly done; but it does not hold him long in this condition, because he could not remain in it and live. Then the Soul, enlightened, inflamed with divine love, and filled with sweetness and delight, exclaims:

Soul. O love, the Soul that feels thee, begins even in this world to possess eternal life; but thou, Lord, dost conceal this work even from its possessor, lest he should spoil it by making it his own. O love, he who feels thee understands thee not; he who desires to comprehend thee cannot know thee. O love, our life, our blessedness, our rest! Divine love brings with it every good and banishes every evil. O heart, wounded with divine love, thou art forever incurable, and dying of this sweet wound, thou dost enter upon never-ending life. O fire of love, what doest thou in man? Thou purifiest him as gold is purified by fire, and dost conduct him with thee to that country and that end for which he was created.

Love is a divine flame: and as material fire ever burns and consumes, according to its nature, so in man the love of God is by its nature ever working toward its end, and for its part never ceases to benefit and serve him whom it holds so dear; he who does not know its power has but himself to blame, since God never tires of doing good to man while he is in this life, and has always the most tender love for him.

O love, I can no longer be silent, and yet I cannot speak as I desire of thy sweet and gentle operation, for I am filled with love which inspires me with the wish to speak but deprives me of the power. Within myself I speak with the heart and with the mind, but when I would pronounce the words, something checks me, and I find myself betrayed by this poor tongue. I would be silent but I cannot, for still the instinct for speech urges me on. If I could utter that love of which my heart is full, I think that every other heart would be inflamed, however remote from love it might be. Before I leave this life I long to speak once of this love, to speak of it as I feel it within me, of its effects in me, and of what it requires of him into whom it is infused, and whom it fills to overflowing with a sweetness above all sweetness, and

227

with an indescribable content, so great that for it one would willingly be burned alive; for God unites a certain zeal with this love, by the power of which man disregards all contradictions how great soever.

O love, powerful and sweet, happy is he who is possessed by thee, for thou dost strengthen, defend, and preserve him from all ills of body and soul. Thou gently guidest all things to their end, and never dost abandon man. Thou art ever faithful, thou givest light against the deceit of the devil, the malice of the world, and against ourselves, who are so full of self and so perverse. This love is so illuminative and efficacious that it draws all imperfections from their secret caverns, that we may apply the remedy and purge ourselves from them.

This love, which rules and governs our will, in order that it may grow strong and firm to resist temptation, so occupies the affections and the intellect that they desire naught beside. The memory is engrossed, and the powers of the soul are satisfied, so that love remains her sole possessor and inhabitant, and she allows nothing else to enter there. Love exhales a continual sweet perfume, by which man suffers himself to be allured, and so powerful is this fragrance that however great may be the torments through which he passes to salvation, there is no martyrdom he would not suffer gladly to attain it.

O love, no words of mine can express the sweetness and delight with which thou fillest the heart; it remains enclosed within, and by speaking it is inflamed. Whoever hears or reads these words without the sentiment of love, makes little account of them, and they pass by him like the wind. But if I could express the joy, the pleasure, and the peace which it brings to the beloved heart, all men who hear or read these words would surrender without resistance. For it is so adapted to the human heart that at its first touch it opens wide its door, although man never can receive this celestial gift till he is free from every other love. If the heart receives but the smallest drop, it so earnestly desires to increase it that it rates as nothing all the goods of this world. With this love, man conquers the evil habits which are a hindrance to him, and in its strength he stands ever ready to perform great deeds.

CHAPTER V

Other effects of love.—What it accomplishes at its will.—The work is all its own.—Of works wrought through love, in love, and by love, with some explanation of them.

O love, with thy sweetness thou breakest the heart that is harder than adamant, and meltest it like wax in the fire. O love, thou makest great men to esteem themselves as the least of the earth, and the richest as the poorest. O love, thou causest wise men to appear as fools, and thou takest their knowledge from the learned and givest them an understanding surpassing all other understanding. O love, thou banishest from the heart all melancholy, hardness, and natural inclinations, and all delight in worldly things. O love, thou makest bad men good, and artful men simple. Thou dost ingeniously deprive men of their free will, so that they are contented to be guided by thee alone, because thou art our guide.

O love, thine operations are alien to this earth; and therefore thou changest man from earthly to celestial, and, depriving him of every human mode of operation, dost unfit him for all earthly occupations. O love, thou dost accomplish the whole work of our salvation, which we neither know how to do nor are able to do without thee. O love, thy name is so sweet that it imparts sweetness to all things. Sweet is the mouth that names thee, most of all when the words proceed from a heart full of thy liquid sweetness, which makes man benign, meek, gracious, joyous, bountiful, and ready, so far as may be, to serve all men. O love, when by any way thou art able to penetrate the heart of man with thy sweet and gracious darts, if it be unoccupied by any other love, however slight may be thy flame, it is powerful enough to make him abandon all things else for thee.

This love makes every affliction and contradiction appear sweet. O love, what sweet quiet, and what quiet sweetness thou bringest with thee! As thou belongest to all, the more thou art diffused among creatures, so much the more fully is thy will accomplished; the more man feels and comprehends thy gentle warmth, the more he is inflamed with desire, and he neither asks for any proof beyond his own feeling, nor knows how to give any other reason for it: but love carries with it its own reason, and the will likewise, and remains lord of the whole man, subjecting him entirely to its will according to its pleasure, and this work is wholly its own; for then its operations are effected through love, in love, and by love.

By works done through love, those works are understood which man performs through the love of God, when God gives him an instinctive desire to work for the benefit of himself or his neighbor; in this first state of love, God causes man to undertake many and various useful and necessary works, which he performs with a pious intention. The works of the second state of love are done in God; these are such as are done with no view either to the advantage of one's self or of one's neighbor, but rest in God, with no motive in him who does them. Here man perseveres in good works through the habits of virtue which he has formed, although God has deprived him of that share in them which gave him aid and pleasure. This work is more perfect than the other, for in that there were many motives which nourished both soul and body. The works done by love are more perfect than the other two, because man has no part whatever in them; love has so subdued and conquered him that he finds himself drowned in the sea of love, and knows not where he is, but is lost in himself and left without the power to act. In this case it is love itself which works in man, and its works are works of perfection, inasmuch as they are not wrought by human power, and are works of sanctifying grace, and God accepts them all.

This sweet and pure love takes possession of man, absorbs him and deprives him of himself. It keeps possession of him and continually works within him, solely for his benefit and advantage, and without any thought or care on his part.

O love, what a sweet companion and faithful guide art thou! Neither speech nor thought can do justice to thy excellence. Blessed is the heart possessed and occupied by thee. Love makes men just, simple, pure, rich, wise, and contented, and with its sweetness lessens every grief.

O love, all that is done through thee is done with ease, with gladness and goodwill; and though the toil be great, thy sweetness tempers every trial. Oh, the torment of working without love! It is beyond belief. Love gives a sweet flavor to every viand. if it is bad it makes it good, and if good it makes it better. According to the grade and the capacity of the subject, God infuses love into the heart of man.

Oh, how sweet a thing it would be to speak of this love, if fitting words were found to express the delight with which it fills the heart. But because the Soul is immortal, and capable of greater love than it can feel in this life, on account of the weakness of the body, which does not allow the Soul to support all that it desires, it remains ever craving, and in this life can never be fully satisfied.

O love, thou fillest the heart, but thou art so great that it cannot contain thee; it remains filled but not satisfied: by the road of his heart thou takest possession of the entire man and permittest none but thyself to find entrance; with a strong bond thou bindest all the facilities of soul and body. O sweet servitude of love, which gives man freedom and contentment in this life, and eternal blessedness in the other!

O love, thy bonds are so sweet and so strong that they bind angels and saints together, and so firm and close that they are never broken; men who are bound by this chain are so united that they have but one will and one aim, and all things among them are in common, both temporal and spiritual. In this union there is no difference between rich, and poor, between nation and nation; all contradiction is excluded, for by this love crooked things are made straight and difficulties reconciled.

CHAPTER VI

The Soul asks various questions of our Lord.—What the martyrs have suffered for this love.—That charity is the shortest and most secure road to salvation, and that without it the Soul would rather cast itself into a thousand hells than enter the presence of God.

O sweet Jesus, my Love, what has brought thee from heaven to earth? Love. What has caused thee to suffer such great and terrible torments, even unto death? Love. What has induced thee to give thyself as food to thy beloved Soul? Love. What moved thee to send us, what still continually moves thee to send us, the Holy Spirit for our support and guide? Love.

Many other things can be said of thee. Through love thou didst appear in this world so poor, so abject, and so humiliated in the eyes of men, that thou wast not esteemed a God, but scarcely as a man. A servant, however faithful and loving, could not endure so much for his master, even were he to promise him heaven itself, because without that interior love which thou bestowest upon man he cannot patiently suffer any torment either of soul or body.

But thou, Lord, hast brought from heaven the sweet manna, this delicious food, which has in itself such vigor that it gives strength for every trial: as we have witnessed first in thee, our most sweet Master, and afterwards in thy saints. Oh, how much they have done and suffered in the strength of the love infused by thee into their hearts, and by which they were so inflamed and united to thee, that no torture could separate them from thee! For in the midst of their torments a zeal was kindled that increased with their sufferings, and by it they were kept from yielding to the most cruel martyrdoms that tyrants could invent.

The spectators saw only the weakness of the body, but the sweet and powerful love which God infused into the heart, and which is so vital and strong that he who abandons himself to it can never be lost, was hidden from them.

There is no briefer or securer way of salvation than this sweet nuptial robe of charity, which gives such confidence and vigor to the Soul that she enters the presence of God without misgiving. But if at death she is found destitute of charity, she is left in such an abject and wretched condition that she would seek the gloomiest and most wretched spot, rather than appear in the divine presence. For God, who is simple and pure, can receive into himself nothing but pure and simple love; and being a sea of love in which all the saints are plunged, it is impossible that even the slightest imperfection should enter therein: hence the Soul, naked of charity when she is separated from the body (aware of her condition), would cast herself into hell rather than approach so bright and pure a presence.

O pure love! Every stain of evil, even the least, is a great hell to thee, and even, by reason of thy vehemence, mere cruel that that of the damned. None but those who have experienced thee can understand and believe this. This love of which I speak, although in itself infinite, can be described in its gracious and familiar action in the beloved Soul, even as if it were one with her.

CHAPTER VII

Our Lord questions the Soul concerning the love she feels and on what he has said to her.—The Soul responds according to her ability, but cannot express the intensity of her love.—She asks our Lord how the loving Soul can live on earth, and concerning her condition.

The Lord. What hast thou to say, O my Soul, of this sweet love, so dear to thee, which never leaves thee to thyself, is always speaking to thee comforting thee, inflaming thee, and revealing to thee some new and celestial beauty, that so thy affection for it may become more and more ardent? Tell me some of those loving words it speaks to thee when thou art with it alone.

Soul. I find myself repeating certain words which are understood in the depths of my heart, which is glowing with an amorous flame. These words, and this sentiment of love, I do not understand and am unable to express, for they are unlike other words. Love opens my heart and is ever making such gracious communications to it that it is wholly inflamed and dissolved in love; yet in particular can discern neither words, flames, nor love; the heart is seized, possessed, and held fast by a loving satisfaction.

Yet the Soul does not comprehend this work, although she perceives that in this visitation, love bestows all possible caresses upon the beloved Soul that a true lover can give when his affection is the greatest that can be conceived. This operation melts the Soul, detaches her from earth, purifies her, makes her simple, strengthens her, and draws her deeper and deeper into its loving flame. But she is not allowed to remain long in this great and penetrating fire, for humanity could not endure its vehemence; yet in the heart there remains always the impression that she is living in that love with God.

O love! thou absorbest this heart into thyself and leavest Humanity deserted on the earth, where it finds no resting place. It appears an exiled creature, with no object either in heaven or in this world.

O love, how burning and enamored is this Soul in which thou art performing such a work of love! I would that I knew how this creature lives upon the earth, both as to her body and her Soul, and how it is that she has her conversation as well with heaven as with creatures; I see her living a life very different from that of others, and one more for admiration than for edification. She sets no value upon anything: she appears like the mistress of heaven and the queen of earth, although she has nothing of her own; few can understand her; she is very free and fearless, and dreads not that anything can ever be wanting to her; she has nothing, and yet, to her seeming, all things are hers.

The Lord. The answer is not for men, blind and deprived of celestial light, who having their intellects occupied with earthly things, cannot comprehend my words; yet, I will answer for those who, aided by the divine ray, will be able to understand it. My love so delights the Soul that it destroys every other joy which can be possessed by man here below. The taste of me extinguishes every other taste; my light blinds all who behold it; all the facilities of the Soul are so possessed and bound by love that she is lost and understands neither what she has done nor what she should do. She is raised above herself and bereft of reason, memory, and will.

Creatures like these no longer take part in the things of this world, save through necessity, and then as if they knew them not. They are always occupied interiorly, and this prevents their being nourished by temporal things. God sends into their hearts rays and flames of love so subtle and penetrating that they know not where they are, but remain silently plunged in the serene depths of that love. And if God did not sometimes deprive them of this vehement love, the Soul could not remain in the body; yet, when he thus departs, he leaves the Soul so sweetly occupied in him that naught beside is seen, known, or understood. Rarely does she remember anything but what she has felt, and until the impression grows weaker it is impossible for her to think of her own affairs, however pressing they may be.

CHAPTER VIII

Of the condition of the loving Soul.—How God delays imparting to her the knowledge of her defects, since she could not endure it.—She has no repose so long as she suspects the existence of any fault by which her Spirit is hindered of its satisfaction.

The state of the Soul is this: she is very sensitive, so that her mind cannot endure the least suspicion of defect, because pure love cannot remain where there is even the slightest fault, and the loving Soul, unable to endure it, would be thrown into intolerable pain. In this world man cannot be wholly free from imperfections, but at times God keeps him in ignorance of them, because he could not support the sight; at other times he reveals them all; and in this way man is purified.

If a suspicion of sin falls upon this Soul, she cannot be pacified nor at rest until her mind is satisfied. The Soul which dwells in that amorous peace cannot be disturbed either by herself or by others; if any misunderstanding arises between herself and another, she is unquiet until she has done all in her power to remove it. And when souls habituated to divine love are, for any cause, permitted by God to be disturbed, for the time they are wretched at being cast out of the tranquil paradise in which they are accustomed to abide; and if God did not return them to their accustomed state it would be impossible for them to live. They live in great liberty and take little heed of earthly things. They are in a manner taken out of themselves, especially as they near the close of this life, of which they are stripped remaining immersed in that love into which the Soul has already found by long experience that God, by the operation of his gracious love, has taken both Soul and body, so that he allows them to want for nothing.

God shows the Soul also, that all the benefits bestowed on her by creatures (whether spiritual or temporal) are given because God moves them to it; and hence she learns to take no heed of creatures, what service soever they may have rendered her, for she perceives clearly that it is God who has done it by the action of his providence. By this vision the Soul is more and more inflamed, and finally abandons herself to love, casting aside all creatures, and finding in God such fullness that she can regard nothing else but him.

And although such a Soul may seem to have some affection for exterior things, do not believe it. It is impossible that any love should enter into hearts like these, except the love of God, unless God himself permits it by reason of some necessity either of the soul or the body. And should this occur, all love and care, coming from such a source, would be no impediment, and would not touch the depths of the heart; but would only be ordered of God for some necessity, because it is needful that pure love should be free from every exterior and interior concern; for, where the Spirit of God is, there is liberty.

O that we could behold this sweet correspondence, and hear those burning words with their joyous vigor, where one can distinguish neither God nor man, but the heart remains in such a state that it seems a little paradise, given by God to souls that are dear to him, as a foretaste of that true and glorious paradise, but hidden from all except those lovers who are absorbed and lost in the ocean of divine love.

O love! the heart which thou possessest becomes through peace of mind so great and so magnanimous, that it would rather suffer martyrdom to gain thee than without thee to be in possession of every other good in heaven or earth. Yet, this is beyond the comprehension of all who have not felt and tasted thee. A heart which finds itself in God sees all created things beneath itself, not through pride or conceit of self, but by reason of its union with God, which makes all that is God's appear to be its own, and beside him it sees, know, and comprehends nothing.

A heart enamored of God is unconquerable, for God is its strength; hell does not affright it nor heaven allure it, for it is so disposed that it receives all that befalls as from the hand of God, remaining with him in immovable peace, and inwardly strengthened and fortified by him.

Soul. O Love! how namest thou these beloved souls?

The Lord. I have said, Ye are gods, and all children of the Most High (Psalm 81).

Soul. O Love! thou annihilatest thy lovers in themselves, and then restorest them to a true and perfect liberty, and makest them masters of themselves. They wish nothing but what God wishes and finds all things else a grave impediment to them.

O Love! I find no words to express thy benign and joyous sway, thy strong and assured freedom, thy sweet and gentle goodness: but all that thy true lover could express would be unequal to what he would desire to say. He seeks everywhere for loving words appropriate to that love, and finds them nowhere; for love and its effects are infinite, and the tongue is not only finite but very feeble, and is always dissatisfied and confused by its powerlessness to say what it desires. And although all that he says is as nothing, yet when man speaks of this love as he feels it in his heart, it relieves him that so he may not die of love. What sayest thou, my Lord, of this thy beloved Soul, who is so enamored of thee?

The Lord. That she is wholly mine. And thou, my Soul, what sayest thou of thy heart?

Soul. That I am wounded, O my God, with love, in which I live joyful and at peace.

CHAPTER IX

Of the condition of the Body, and in what suffering Humanity found itself, living as though dead.—How God provided for it.— Of the joy experienced by the Soul in the interchange of love, and how she is left like one dead when deprived of it.

As the state of a Soul enkindled and glowing with divine love has been explained, something now remains to be said of the condition of the body. The body cannot live on love, like the Soul, but it is nourished by material food. And as God has willed to separate the Soul from earthly things and from her body, and engage her wholly in spiritual operations, therefore it is left without vigor and almost without nourishment, for all communication having ceased between it and the Soul, without which it has no strength, it becomes like a Soul deprived of God, like one dead, without enjoyment, without vigor, and without aid or comfort. And if God should for a long time keep the Soul thus vehemently occupied within herself, it would be impossible in the nature of things for the body to survive.

But God, who sees all things, provides for all necessities, and although, by reason of the union of the Soul with God, Humanity has little comfort, and can neither smile, nor relish food, nor sleep, nor take delight in the emotions of the Soul or the sensations of the body, nor in any earthly thing, yet God concedes it a sufficiency for the support of its wearisome life. And in order that every imperfection which exists in man may die in God (while man still lives upon the earth), God seems to open a vein and let out the blood of Humanity, the Soul meanwhile remaining as if in a bath, and when there is no more blood within the body, and the Soul is wholly transformed in God, then each goes to its own place, the Soul to her rest in God and the body to the grave; and this work is done in secret and by love alone. If you know how harassed and besieged is this poor Humanity, you would in truth believe that no creature suffers so greatly as itself; but because this is invisible it is neither credited nor understood, nor has any one compassion for it, especially as it is endured for the love of God. But I say (with all this for the love of God), it is necessary that this creature should live always as if dead, like a man hanging by his feet, who, notwithstanding, lives. And though it may be said, and truly, that the heart is contented, yet what enjoyment can the body have? Thus Humanity, no longer able to live according to its nature, appears to me to be always tortured and greatly afflicted. It lives, but knows not how it lives, nor on what food. It desires nothing, but remains in God, who pierces often this beloved heart with darts of love so keen that they almost destroy the body by the ardor of their penetrating and amorous flame, and absorbs the Soul in an obscure and hidden satisfaction from which she would never part, since in it she finds her own proper repose and natural beatitude, which God often reveals to the heart he loves.

But the body, constrained to follow the Soul (without which it cannot live or do aught, not being Spirit), remains during this time as if without a Soul and without human comfort, in almost mortal weakness, and knows not how to aid itself. Therefore in this necessity it is assisted by others or secretly provided for by God himself, for otherwise this creature would be as helpless as a little child, who having no one to care for it, can do nothing but weep until its wants are supplied. It is not to be wondered at, therefore, that for creatures like this, God should provide particular persons to assist them, by whose means all their necessities both of Soul and body are supplied, for otherwise they would die. Behold how our Lord Jesus Christ left his beloved Mother to the special care of St. John; he did the same for his disciples, and does it still for other devout persons; in such a manner that one succors another both in spiritual and temporal things with this divine union. And because people in general do not understand these operations, and have no such union, therefore particular persons are needed for such cares, through whom God may operate by his grace and light.

Those who behold such creatures and do not understand them, admire, rather than are edified by them; do not judge them, then, if you do not wish to err. But consider how besieged and how afflicted is this Humanity, living as if without life. She lives because God gives her the grace to live; but by nature her life would be impossible. When the Soul was able to give love for love, that love yielded Humanity a certain satisfaction which sustained it; but now, when the Soul is deprived of all sensible and active love, Humanity is left abandoned and forsaken, like one dead. But God performs another loving work, so secret and so subtle that the Soul becomes more noble and more perfect than before, by reason of the destitution and the nakedness in which God leaves her, so that without other support she rests, firm and stable, on him alone.

CHAPTER X

How the Soul, the heart, and the Spirit of this creature are devoid of form, and employed in an occupation which cannot be known by their means.—That the heart becomes the tabernacle of God, into which he infuses many graces and consolations, which produce admirable fruits.—That few creatures are led by this road.—Of the nudity of the Spirit and of its union with God.

The Lord. What will you do, O Soul, thus naked and despoiled? What will you do, O heart and mind, which are both so empty? How is it with you in this state, before unknown to you?

Soul. I know not where I am; I have lost will, understanding, memory, love, and all enjoyment; I can give no reason for myself, and am lost, and can neither place myself nor seek or find any other thing.

The heart and the mind of this creature being deprived of all the ways by means of which heaven seemed to make an entrance, now exclaim: We are absorbed in an operation too subtle and secret to be made known by us, but in that occupation a loving and ethereal spirit is hidden and restrained which fills the whole man so entirely, that Soul, heart, mind, and body, every bone and nerve and vein, are overflowing with it, so that all are absorbed with such a secret and concentrated force, that every sigh struggling from the heart is felt interiorly as a vehement flame. But the body, unable to endure the action of so powerful a flame, grieves, yet finds no words to express its grief; the mouth is filled with burning sighs and amorous conceits, which rise from the heart, and seem ready to break forth in words powerful enough to break a heart of stone. But they find no utterance; the true and loving colloquy is going on within, and its sweetness cannot be conceived. The heart is made the tabernacle of God, into which, by himself and also by others, many graces are infused, which bear in secret wondrous fruits. This creature has a heaven within herself.

If such as she (and they are rare in this world) were understood, they would be adored upon earth; but God hides them from themselves and from all others until the hour of death, at which time the true and false are made known. Oh, how few creatures are conducted by this road of secret and penetrating love, which keeps both Soul and body in such subjection that it leaves no imperfection in them, for pure love can comport with none, however slight; and it perseveres in its sweet action in the Soul until it purifies her entirely, so that she can reach her proper end without passing through purgatory.

O Soul, O mind, bound and imprisoned in that divine flame! who could comprehend that beauty, that wisdom, that amorous care wrought in you by divine love and for love—those colloquies so sweet, so loving, and so gracious—and not feel his heart melt within him, though it were harder than a stone.

O love! thou art called love until all that love is perfected which God has infused into the heart of man, in which he rests inebriated and immersed until he knows no longer what love is; for then it becomes Spirit and unites with the Spirit of man, so that he becomes spiritual. And the Spirit, being invisible and inscrutable to all the powers of the Soul, man is conquered and subdued, and knows no longer where he is, where he should be, nor whither he should go. But by reason of this secret and intimate union with God, there remains in the Soul a sweet impression, so firm and assured a satisfaction, that no torture, however cruel, could overpower it, and a zeal so ardent that a man, had he a thousand lives, would risk them all for that hidden consciousness which is so strong that hell itself could not destroy it. O Spirit, naked and invisible, none is able to lay hold of thee, by reason of thy nakedness! Thy habitation is in heaven, albeit with thy body thou yet remainest on the earth. Thou knowest not thyself, nor art thou known by others in this world. All thy lovers and thy kindred who are in heaven are known to thee only by virtue of an interior instinct implanted within thee by the Spirit of God.

O that I could find words fitting to describe that gracious friendship and that vanished union. Vanished, I say, because so far as man is concerned he has lost completely all expressions, that is, of love, union, annihilation, transformation, sweetness, softness, goodness; has lost, in short, all forms of speech by means of which the absolute union of two separate things could be expressed and comprehended, where nothing remains but one pure Spirit, active, and simple, and incomprehensible.

CHAPTER XI

Of the secret means used by God for the purification of man.—
Of the loving care he takes of him.—How he sweetly leads him
by love, and does not allow him to work for his own advan-
tage.—That true nakedness of spirit cannot be expressed by
words.

O sweetest, my Lord, in how many hidden ways thou workest in man when thou desirest to purify him by means of thy most pure love, which removes all rust from the Soul and prepares it for the most holy union with thee! Oh, vast and happy country, unknown to wretched mortals, but for which they were created by God!

O infinite God, how is it possible that thou shouldst not be known and loved by him whom thou hast made capable of knowing and enjoying thee, unless solely by reason of the little taste and feeling which by thy grace thou hast bestowed upon him! For, if in this world man possessed thee, he would leave all things beside.

O Lord, what loving care thou takest, day and night, of man, who knoweth not himself, and much less knoweth thee, although thou lovest him so much, seekest him with such diligence, and waitest for and bearest him with so much patience, out of thy divine love!

Thou art that great most high God of whom we can neither speak nor think, because of the ineffable supereminence of thy glory, wisdom, power, and infinite goodness: and all these thou employest in the service of man, who is so vile, but whom thou wouldst make so great and worthy; and therefore thou art ever luring him with thy love because thou art unwilling to force the free-will which thou hast given him. Thou drawest him to thee by love, and desirest that he consent to thee through love. Thou workest in him by love and with thy love. Thou wouldst have the whole man act through love, that so, without thy love he might do nothing. Thou, who art our God and Lord, hast disregarded thine own ease, both of soul and body, that thou mightest save man; and thou willest that he also should disregard all ease of soul and body that he may do thy will: and this chiefly because thy will is our best good: but this, by blind and miserable man is never understood.

I have not spoken well of the nakedness of the Spirit. It is because there are no words by which this nakedness might be expressed, and the soul which finds herself in that condition has in her mind a fullness, a repletion, of which she knows not how to speak: and yet by reason of the vehemence of her emotions she is forced to speak, and in a language more fitting than she is aware. This language is like the ink, black and unseemly, and yet by its means many thoughts are made plain which could not otherwise be understood.

Alas! if man could comprehend what it is that the mind feels in such a state, these words would indeed appear to him dark and unseemly. What, then, are these hearts and tongues to do which cannot utter their thoughts? So secret and hidden are they that to him who feels them it seems impossible that he should find any who can understand, and much less express them. Will he then remain silent wonder? No, for he is unable to be silent, finding his heart ever more inflamed by the marvelous operations of divine love, which God increased day by day within him, and which bind him so closely by the invisible chains of love that Humanity can hardly endure it, more especially when it sees the madness of men, who are so wrapped in exterior things that they neither know, conjecture, nor comprehend this divine operation. But God loves us so much that although he sees us so blind and deaf to our own advantage, yet he does not for that reason cease to knock continually at our hearts by his holy inspirations, that so he may enter and make therein tabernacles for himself into which creatures can never enter more.

CHAPTER XII

Exclamations of the Soul upon the blindness which creatures offer to the love of God.—Of the secret operations of God in man, arousing and admonishing him with love.—The Soul inquires concerning this work, and desires to know what grace is, and what is the ray of love.

Alas! how few and rare are they in whom God abides by these operations! O God, thou retainest thy love within thyself because thou canst not infuse it into creatures so occupied with earthly affairs.

O earth, earth, what wilt thou do with those whom thou dost so absorb? The Soul lost and the body corrupted, all things are lost in infinite and incredible torments. Reflect upon this, O Soul! Reflect, and no longer lose the time and the power which are now given thee to escape all danger; thy God is now gracious and propitious to thee. He is very anxious for thy salvation, and is ever seeking and calling thee with measureless love. The operations which God is continually working on our behalf are so many and great, that they can neither be recounted nor imagined: but all the good which he has done to us, is still doing, will do, and desires to do, will result in our condemnation and our confusion if we fail to cooperate with him in the time which we so undervalue.

Soul. Show me, O my Lord, if it please thee, how thou dost work within man by thy secret love, in which he is taken captive by thee, not knowing how, nor understanding in what manner, but only finding himself a prisoner of love and greatly satisfied.

The Lord. I move with my love the heart of man, and with that movement give him light by which he sees that I am inspiring him to well-doing; and in that light he ceases to do ill, and struggles with his evil inclinations.

Soul. What is this movement, and how does it begin in man, who knows not of its existence and asks not for it?

The Lord. The pure, simple, and boundless love which I bear toward all men, impels me to grant him this grace, to knock at his heart, to see whether he will open and give me entrance, that so I may make my abode there and banish all things else.

Soul. And what is this grace?

The Lord. It is an inspiration which I send him by means of a ray of love, with which I give him also the instinct of love; it is impossible for him not to love, and although he knows not what he loves, yet he learns it by little and little.

Soul. What is the ray of love?

The Lord. Behold the rays of the sun, which are so subtle and penetrating that human eyes cannot behold them without losing their sight; such are the rays of my love which I send into human hearts, and which deprive man of all knowledge and all delight in worldly things.

Soul. And these rays, how do they enter into the hearts of men?

The Lord. Like darts directed at this one and at that; they touch the heart in secret, inflame it, and make it heave with sighs; man knows not what he wishes, but finding himself wounded with love can give no account of his condition, and remains lost in wonder.

Soul. And what is this dart?

The Lord. It is a scintillation of love which I infuse into man, which softens his obduracy and melts him as wax is melted by the fire. I give him also the instinct to refer to me all the love which I infuse.

Soul. And what is this scintillation?

The Lord. It is an inspiration sent by me which sets on fire the human heart, and so ardently and powerfully inflames it, that it can do nothing but love. By its power man is kept constantly intent on me, and is continually admonished by it within his heart.

What this interior inspiration is, which works so secretly, cannot be told in words. Ask of the heart which feels it. Ask of the intellect which understands it. Ask of the mind filled with the operations which God effects by means of it, for the least conception that can be formed of it is that given by the tongue. God fills man with love; he draws him to himself by love, and by its force enables him to overcome the world, the devils, and himself; but man cannot understand this love nor put it into words.

CHAPTER XIII

That love cannot be comprehended, and that the heart filled with
it lives content.—Of the great mercy which God shows man in
this life.—That his justice becomes apparent at the moment when
the Soul leaves the body and passes to its destined place.—That
the Soul can find repose in God only.

O my heart, what sayest thou of this love? What kindest
thou? I say: My words are an interior jubilee, but they have no
appropriate utterance. Neither by exterior signs, nor yet by
sufferings (although endured for the love of God), can this love
be made comprehensible; he only who has felt it can somewhat
understand it. All that can be said of love is nothing, for the
further one advances, the less he knows; but the heart, filled and
satisfied, seeks and desires naught else but what it feels. All his
words are heartfelt, glowing, and delightful, and so penetrating
and in such subtle harmony with that which inspires them, that
they can be comprehended only by those whose hearts are also
united with God. God only comprehends them fully; the heart
feels but understands not, and the work is that of God alone,
while the benefit belongs to man. But the intimate, amorous
relation which God sustains with the heart of man is a secret
between him and the heart.

The Lord. O Soul, what hast thou to say touching this
operation?

Soul. I find my will so strong and my liberty so vivid and so
great, that I fear no impediments between me and my object, and
in it I rest content. My intellect is greatly enlightened and daily
becomes more calm; daily are manifested to it things so new and
processes so delightful, that it is satisfied to remain ever thus
employed, and seek no further since here it finds its rest; but it is

impossible for it to explain these operations. The memory is satisfied to be employed in spiritual things, and can with difficulty recall any others. The affections which are natural to man are overshadowed by a supernatural love, which alone satisfied him, and makes him desire no other food, since in it he finds all that he requires. And yet man can render no account of the way in which he is conquered by an operation surpassing all his powers.

What more shall I say concerning this work of love? I am forced to silence, yet have an instinctive wish to speak, although I cannot speak as I desire. Let him who wishes to experience these things abstain, as St. Paul commands, from every appearance of evil. Whenever man does this, at once God infuses into his soul some gift of grace, which he increases with so much love that the man is lost, absorbed, transformed, and overpowered. And however difficult it may appear to abstain from evil, no one would allow any hindrance to prevent him from doing everything for God, who could see the readiness with which he comes to the help of man, and the loving and watchful care with which he aids him and defends him from his adversaries. But when man has once entered the straight road, he learns that it is God who works all that is good in us, by his gracious inspirations and the love infused into the Soul, which acts without hindrance by reason of the satisfaction which God mingles with all her toils. It is enough for man not to act in contradiction to his conscience, for God inspires all the good he would have us do, and gives the instinct and the strength for it, otherwise man could do no good thing. For this God gives all the facilities and the means, so that he enables us to do all things with pleasure, even those that to others seem the greatest penances.

O how great is the love, the kindness, and the mercy which God shows to man in this wretched world! Justice is made known afterwards at the moment when the soul leaves the body; then, if she has not to undergo purgation, God receives her into himself, where she is transformed by his burning love, and thus

254

transformed remains in him forever. At that moment also she goes to purgatory or to hell, if there is aught within her to be purged or to be punished: this is accomplished by the divine decree which sends each one to his own place. Every one carries within himself his own sentence, and is by himself condemned. If souls did not then find the places ordained for them by God, their torments would be even greater, for they would have violated the divine order; and as there is no place which his mercy does not visit, when they are within his order, their sufferings are less than they would otherwise be. The soul was created by God for himself, and is governed by him, and it can find no repose but in him alone. The condemned in hell are in the order of God through justice. Could they be outside of it they would be in a still greater hell by their violation of the divine order, which gives them the terrible instinct to go directly to their appointed place. Elsewhere their sufferings would be redoubled, and therefore they go thither, not indeed that they may suffer less, but impelled by that supreme and infallible decree of God, which cannot err.

TREATISE ON PURGATORY

The divine fire which St. Catherine experienced in herself, made her comprehend the state of souls in purgatory, and that they are contented there although in torment.

CHAPTER I

The state of souls in purgatory.—They are exempt from all self-love.

This holy soul, while still in the flesh, was placed in the purgatory of the burning love of God, in whose flames she was purified from every stain, so that when she passed from this life she might be ready to enter the presence of God, her most sweet love. By means of that flame of love she comprehended in her own soul the condition of the souls of the faithful in purgatory, where they are purified from the rust and stain of sins, from which they have not been cleansed in this world. And as in the purgatory of that divine flame she was united with the divine love and satisfied with all that was accomplished in her, she was enabled to comprehend the state of the souls in purgatory, and thus discovered concerning it:

"As far as I can see, the souls in purgatory can have no choice but to be there; this God has most justly ordained by his divine decree. They cannot turn towards themselves and say: 'I have committed such and such sins for which I deserve to remain here;' nor can they say: 'Would that I had refrained from them, for then I should at this moment be in paradise;' nor again: 'This soul will be released before me;' or 'I shall be released before her.' They retain no memory of either good or evil respecting themselves or others which would increase their pain.

They are so contented with the divine dispositions in their regard; and with doing all that is pleasing to God in that way which he chooses, that they cannot think of themselves, though they may strive to do so. They see nothing but the operation of the divine goodness which is so manifestly bringing them to God that they can reflect neither on their own profit nor on their hurt. Could they do so, they would not be in pure charity. They see not that they suffer their pains in consequence of their sins, nor can they for a moment entertain that thought, for should they do so it would be an active imperfection, and that cannot exist in a state where there is no longer the possibility of sin. At the moment of leaving this life they see why they are sent to purgatory, but never again, otherwise they would still retain something private, which has no place there. Being established in charity, they can never deviate therefrom by any defect, and have no will or desire, save the pure will of pure love, and can swerve from it in nothing. They can neither commit sin, nor merit by refraining from it.

CHAPTER II

The joy of souls in purgatory.—The saint illustrates their ever increasing vision of God.—The difficulty of speaking about their state.

"There is no peace to be compared with that of the souls in purgatory, save that of the saints in paradise, and this peace is ever augmented by the inflowing of God into these souls, which increases in proportion as the impediments to it are removed. The rust of sin is the impediment, and this the fire continually consumes, so that the soul in this state is continually opening itself to admit the divine communication. As a covered surface can never reflect the sun, not through any defect in that orb, but simply from the resistance offered by the covering, so, if the covering be gradually removed, the surface will by little and little be opened to the sun and will more and more reflect his light.

"So it is with the rust of sin, which is the covering of the soul. In purgatory the flames incessantly consume it, and as it disappears, the soul reflects more and more perfectly the true sun who is God. Its contentment increases as this rust wears away, and the soul is laid bare to the divine ray, and thus one increases and the other decreases until the time is accomplished. The pain never diminishes, although the time does, but as to the will, so united is it to God by pure charity, and so satisfied to be under his divine appointment, that these souls can never say their pains are pains.

"On the other hand, it is true that they suffer torments which no tongue can describe nor any intelligence comprehend, unless it be revealed by such a special grace as that which God has vouchsafed to me, but which I am unable to explain. And this vision which God revealed to me has never departed from my memory. I will describe it as far as I am able, and they whose intellects our Lord will deign to open will understand me.

CHAPTER III

Separation from God is the greatest pain of purgatory.—In this, purgatory differs from hell.

"The source of all suffering is either original or actual sin. God created the soul pure, simple, free from every stain, and with a certain beatific instinct toward himself. It is drawn aside from aim by original sin, and when actual sin is afterwards added, this withdraws it still farther, and ever as it removes from him its sinfulness increases because its communication with God grows less and less.

"And because there is no good except by participation with God, who, to the irrational creatures imparts himself as he wills and in accordance with his divine decree, and never withdraws from them, but to the rational soul he imparts himself more or less, according as he finds her more or less freed from the hindrances of sin, it follows that, when he finds a soul that is returning to the purity and simplicity in which she was created, he increased in her the beatific instinct, and kindles in her a fire of charity so powerful and vehement, that it is insupportable to the soul to find any obstacle between her and her end; and the clearer vision she has of these obstacles the greater is her pain.

"Since the souls in purgatory are freed from the guilt of sin, there is no barrier between them and God save only the pains they suffer, which delay the satisfaction of their desire. And when they see how serious is even the slightest hindrance, which the necessity of justice causes to check them, a vehement flame kindles within them, which is like that of hell. They feel no guilt however, and it is guilt which is the cause of the malignant will of the condemned in hell, to whom God does not communicate his goodness, and thus they remain in despair and with a will forever opposed to the good will of God.

CHAPTER IV

The difference between the state of the souls in hell and that of those in purgatory.—Reflections of the saint upon those who neglect their salvation.

"It is evident that the revolt of man's will from that of God constitutes sin, and while that revolt continues, man's guilt remains. Those, therefore, that are in hell, having passed from this life with perverse wills, their guilt is not remitted, nor can it be, since they are no longer capable of change. When this life is ended, the soul remains forever confirmed either in good or evil according as she has here determined. As it is written: Where I shall find thee, that is, at the hour of death, with the will either fixed on sin or repenting of it, there I will judge thee. From this judgment there is no appeal, for after death the freedom of the will can never return, but the will is confirmed in that state in which it is found at death. The souls in hell, having been found at that hour with the will to sin, have the guilt and the punishment always with them, and although this punishment is not so great as they deserve, yet it is eternal. Those in purgatory, on the other hand, suffer the penalty only, for their guilt was cancelled at death, when they were found hating their sins and penitent for having offended the divine goodness. And this penalty has an end, for the term of it is ever approaching. O misery beyond all misery, and the greater because in his blindness man regards it not!

"The punishment of the damned is not, it is true, infinite in degree, for the all lovely goodness of God shines even into hell. He who dies in mortal sin merits infinite woe for an infinite duration; but the mercy of God has made the time only infinite, and mitigated the intensity of the pain. In justice he might have inflicted much greater punishment than he has done.

"Oh, what peril attaches to sin willfully committed! For it is so difficult for man to bring himself to penance, and without penitence guilt remains and will ever remain, so long as man retains unchanged the will to sin, or is intent upon committing it.

CHAPTER V

Of the peace and joy which are found in purgatory

"The souls in purgatory are entirely conformed to the will of God; therefore, they correspond with his goodness, are contented with all that he ordains, and are entirely purified from the guilt of their sins. They are pure from sins, because they have in this life abhorred them and confessed them with true contrition, and for this reason God remits their guilt, so that only the stains of sin remain, and these must be devoured by the fire. Thus freed from guilt and united to the will of God, they see him clearly according to that degree of light which he allows them, and comprehend how great a good is the fruition of God, for which all souls were created. Moreover, these souls are in such close conformity to God, and are drawn so powerfully toward him by reason of the natural attraction between him and the soul, that no illustration or comparison could make this impetuosity understood in the way in which my spirit conceives it by its interior sense. Nevertheless I will use one which occurs to me.

CHAPTER VI

A comparison to express with how great violence of love the souls in purgatory desire to enjoy God.

"Let us suppose that in the whole world there were but one loaf to appease the hunger of every creature, and that the bare sight of it would satisfy them. Now man, when in health, has by nature the instinct for food, but if we can suppose him to abstain from it and neither die nor yet lose health and strength, his hunger would clearly become increasingly urgent. In this case, if he knew that nothing but the loaf would satisfy him, and that until he reached it his hunger could not be appeased, he would suffer intolerable pains, which would increase as his distance from the loaf diminished; but if he were sure that he would never see it, his hell would be as complete as that of the damned souls, who, hungering after God, have no hope of ever seeing the bread of life. But the souls in purgatory have an assured hope of seeing him and of being entirely satisfied; and therefore they endure all hunger and suffer all pain until that moment when they enter into eternal possession of this bread, which is Jesus Christ, our Lord, our Savior, and our Love.

CHAPTER VII

Of the marvelous wisdom of God in the creation of purgatory and of hell.

"As the purified spirit finds no repose but in God, for whom it was created, so the soul in sin can rest nowhere but in hell, which by, reason of its sins, has become its end. Therefore, at that instant in which the soul separates from the body, it goes to its prescribed place, needing no other guide than the nature of the sin itself, if the soul has parted from the body in mortal sin. And if the soul were hindered from obeying that decree (proceeding from the justice of God), it would find itself in a yet deeper hell, for it would be outside of the divine order, in which mercy always finds place and prevents the full infliction of all the pains the soul has merited. Finding, therefore, no spot more fitting, nor any in which her pains would be so slight, she casts herself into her appointed place.

"The same thing is true of purgatory: the soul, leaving the body, and not finding in herself that purity in which she was created, and seeing also the hindrances which prevent her union with God, conscious also that purgatory only can remove them, casts herself quickly and willingly therein. And if she did not find the means ordained for her purification, she would instantly create for herself a hell worse than purgatory, seeing that by reason of this impediment she is hindered from approaching her end, which is God; and this is so great an ill that in comparison with it the soul esteems purgatory as nothing. True it is, as I have said, like hell; and yet, in comparison with the loss of God it is as nothing.

CHAPTER VIII

Of the necessity of purgatory, and of its terrific character

"I will say furthermore: I see that as far as God is concerned, paradise has no gates, but he who will may enter. For God is all mercy, and his open arms are ever extended to receive us into his glory. But I see that the divine essence is so pure—purer than the imagination can conceive—that the soul, finding in itself the slightest imperfection, would rather cast itself into a thousand hells than appear, so stained, in the presence of the divine majesty. Knowing, then, that purgatory was intended for her cleaning, she throws herself therein, and finds there that great mercy, the removal of her stains.

"The great importance of purgatory, neither mind can conceive nor tongue describe. I see only that its pains are as great as those of hell; and yet I see that a soul, stained with the slightest fault, receiving this mercy, counts its pains as naught in comparison with this hindrance to her love. And I know that the greatest misery of the souls in purgatory is to behold in themselves aught that displeases God, and to discover that, in spite of his goodness, they had consented to it. And this is because, being in the state of grace, they see the reality and the importance of the impediments which hinder their approach to God.

CHAPTER IX

How God and the soul reciprocally regard each other in purgatory.—The saint confesses that she has no words to express these things.

"All these things that I have said, in comparison with those which have been represented to my mind (as far as I have been able to comprehend them in this life), are of such magnitude that every idea, every word, every feeling, every imagination, all the justice and all the truth that can be said of them, seem false and worthless, and I remain confounded at the impossibility of finding words to describe them.

"I behold such a great conformity between God and the soul, that when he finds her pure as when his divine majesty first created her he gives her an attractive force of ardent love which would annihilate her if she were not immortal. He so transforms her into himself that, forgetting all, she no longer sees aught beside him; and he continues to draw her toward him, inflames her with love, and never leaves her until he has brought her to that state from whence she first came forth, that is, to the perfect purity in which she was created.

"When the soul beholds within herself the amorous flame by which she is drawn toward her sweet Master and her God, the burning heat of love overpowers her and she melts. Then, in that divine light she sees how God, by his great care and constant providence, never ceases to attract her to her last perfection, and that he does so through pure love alone. She sees, too, that she herself, clogged by sin, cannot follow that attraction toward God, that is, that reconciling glance which he casts upon her that he may draw her to himself. Moreover, a comprehension of that great misery, which it is to be hindered from gazing upon the light of God, is added to the instinctive desire of the soul to be wholly free to yield herself to that unifying flame. I repeat, it is the view of all these things which causes the pain of the suffering souls in purgatory, not that they esteem their pains as great (cruel thought they be), but they count as far worse that opposition which they find in themselves to the will of that God whom they behold burning for them with so ardent and so pure a love.

"This love, with its unifying regard, is ever drawing these souls, as if it had no other thing to do; and when the soul beholds this, if she could find a yet more painful purgatory in which she could be more quickly cleansed, she would plunge at once therein, impelled by the burning, mutual love between herself and God.

CHAPTER X

How God makes use of purgatory to complete the purification of the soul.—That she acquires therein a purity so great that if she were yet to remain after her purification she would cease to suffer.

"From that furnace of divine love I see rays of fire dart like burning lamps towards the soul; and so violent and powerful are they that both soul and body would be utterly destroyed, if that were possible. These rays perform a double office; they purify and they annihilate.

"Consider gold: the oftener it is melted, the more pure does it become; continue to melt it and every imperfection is destroyed. This is the effect of fire on all materials. The soul, however, cannot be annihilated in God, but in herself she can, and the longer her purification lasts, the more perfectly does she die to herself, until at length she remains purified in God.

"When gold has been completely freed from dross, no fire, however great, has any further action on it, for nothing but its imperfections can be consumed. So it is with the divine fire in the soul. God retains her in these flames until every stain is burned away, and she is brought to the highest perfection of which she is capable, each soul in her own degree. And when this is accomplished, she rests wholly in God. Nothing of herself remains, and God is her entire being. When he has thus led her to himself and purified her, she is no longer passable, for nothing remains to be consumed. If when thus refined she should again approach the fire she would feel no pain, for to her it has become the fire of divine love, which is life eternal and which nothing mars.

CHAPTER XI

The desire of souls in purgatory to be purified from every stain of sin.—The wisdom of God in veiling from them their defects.

"At her creation the soul received all the means of attaining perfection of which her nature was capable, in order that she might conform to the will of God and keep herself from contracting any stain; but being directly contaminated by original sin she loses her gifts and graces and even her life. Nor can she be regenerated save by the help of God, for even after baptism her inclination to evil remains, which, if she does not resist it, disposes and leads her to mortal sin, through which she dies anew.

"God again restores her by a further special grace; yet, she is still so sullied and so bent on herself, that to restore her to her primitive innocence, all those divine operations which I have described are needful, and without them she could never be restored. When the soul has reentered the path which leads to her first estate, she is inflamed with so burning a desire to be transformed into God, that in it she finds her purgatory. Not, indeed, that she regards her purgatory as being such, but this desire, so fiery and so powerfully repressed, becomes her purgatory.

"This final act of love accomplishes its work alone, finding the soul with so many hidden imperfections, that the mere sight of them, were it presented to her, would drive her to despair. This last operation, however, consumes them all, and when they are destroyed God makes them known to the soul to make her understand the divine action by which her purity was restored.

CHAPTER XII

How joy and suffering are united in purgatory

"That which man judges to be perfect, in the sight of God is defect. For all the works of man, which appear faultless when he considers them feels, remembers, wills and understands them, are, if he does not refer them to God, corrupt and sinful. For, to the perfection of our works it is necessary that they be wrought in us but not of us. In the works of God it is he that is the prime mover, and not man.

"These works, which God effects in the soul by himself alone, which are the last operations of pure and simple love in which we have no merit, so pierce and inflame the soul that the body which envelops her seems to be hiding a fire, or like one in a furnace, who can find no rest but death. It is true that the divine love which overwhelms the soul gives, as I think, a peace greater than can be expressed; yet this peace does not in the least diminish her pains, nay, it is love delayed which occasions them, and they are greater in proportion to the perfection of the love of which God has made her capable.

"Thus have these souls in purgatory great pleasure and great pain; nor does the one impede the other.

CHAPTER XIII

The souls in purgatory are not in a state to merit.—How they regard the suffrages offered for them in this world.

"If by repentance the souls in purgatory could purify themselves, a moment would suffice to cancel their whole debt, so overwhelming would be the force of the contrition produced by the clear vision they have of the magnitude of every obstacle which hinders them from God, their love and their final end.

"And, know for certain that not one farthing of their debt is remitted to these souls. This is the decree of divine justice; it is thus that God wills. But, on the other hand, these souls have no longer any will apart from that of God, and can neither see nor desire aught but by his appointment.

"And if pious offerings be made for them by persons in this world, they cannot now note them with satisfaction, unless, indeed, in reference to the will of God and the balance of his justice, leaving to him the ordering of the whole, who repays himself as best pleases his infinite goodness. Could they regard these alms apart from the divine will concerning them, this would be a return to self, which would shut from their view the will of God, and that would be to them like hell. Therefore they are unmoved by whatever God gives them, whether it be pleasure or pain, nor can they ever again revert to self.

CHAPTER XIV

Of the submission of the souls in purgatory to the will of God

"So hidden and transformed in God are they, that they rest content with all his holy will. And if a soul, retaining the slightest stain, were to draw near to God in the beatific vision, it would be to her a more grievous injury, and inflict more suffering, than purgatory itself. Nor could God himself, who is pure goodness and supreme justice, and the sight of God, not yet entirely satisfied (so long as the least possible purification remained to be accomplished) would be intolerable to her, and she would cast herself into the deepest hell rather than stand before him and be still impure."

CHAPTER XV

Reproaches of the soul in purgatory to persons in this world

And thus this blessed Soul, illuminated by the divine ray, said: "Would that I could utter so strong a cry that it would strike all men with terror, and say to them: O wretched beings! why are you so blinded by this world that you make, as you will find at the hour of death, no provision for the great necessity that will then come upon you?

"You shelter yourselves beneath your hope in the mercy of God, which you unceasingly exalt, not seeing that it is your resistance to his great goodness which will be your condemnation. His goodness should constrain you to his will, not encourage you to persevere in your own. Since his justice is unfailing it must needs be in some way fully satisfied.

"Have not the boldness to say: 'I will go to confession and gain a plenary indulgence and thus I shall be saved.' Remember that the full confession and entire contrition which are requisite to gain a plenary indulgence are not easily attained. Did you know how hardly they are come by, you would tremble with fear and be more sure of losing than of gaining them.

CHAPTER XVI

Showing that the sufferings of the souls in purgatory do not prevent their peace and joy.

"I see that the souls in purgatory behold a double operation. The first is that of the mercy of God; for while they suffer their torments willingly, they perceive that God has been very good to them, considering what they have deserved and how great are their offences in his eyes. For if his goodness did not temper justice with mercy (satisfying it with the precious blood of Jesus Christ), one sin alone would deserve a thousand hells. They suffer their pains so willingly that they would not lighten them in the least, knowing how justly they have been deserved. They resist the will of God no more than if they had already entered upon eternal life.

"The other operation is that satisfaction they experience in beholding how loving and merciful have been the divine decrees in all that regards them. In one instant God impresses these two things upon their minds, and as they are in grace they comprehend them as they are, yet each according to her capacity. They experience thence a great and never-failing satisfaction which constantly increases as they approach to God. They see all things, not in themselves nor by themselves, but as they are in God, on whom they are more intent than on their sufferings. For the least vision they can have of God overbalances all woes and all joys that can be conceived. Yet their joy in God does by no means abate their pain.

CHAPTER XVII

Which concludes with an application of all that has been said concerning the souls in purgatory to what the saint experiences in her own soul.

"This process of purification to which I see the souls in purgatory subjected, I feel within myself, and have experienced it for the last two years. Every day I see and feel it more clearly. My soul seems to live in this body as in a purgatory which resembles the true purgatory, with only the difference that my soul is subjected to only so much suffering as the body can endure without dying, but which will continually and gradually increase until death.

"I feel my spirit alienated from all things (even spiritual ones) that might afford it nourishment or give it consolation. I have no relish for either temporal or spiritual goods through the will, the understanding, or the memory, nor can I say that I take greater satisfaction in this thing than in that.

"I have been so besieged interiorly, that all things which refreshed my spiritual or my bodily life have been gradually taken from me, and as they departed, I learned that they were all sources of consolation and support. Yet, as soon as they were discovered by the spirit they became tasteless and hateful; they vanish and I care not to prevent it. This is because the spirit instinctively endeavors to rid itself of every hindrance to its perfection, and so resolutely that it would rather go to hell than fail in its purpose. It persists, therefore, in casting off all things by which the inner man might nourish himself, and so jealously guards him, that no slightest imperfection can creep in without being instantly detected and expelled.

"As for the outward man, for the reason that the spirit has no correspondence with it, it is so oppressed that nothing on earth can give it comfort according to its human inclinations. No consolation remains to it but God, who, with great love and mercy accomplishes this work for the satisfaction of his justice. I perceive all this, and it gives me a great peace and satisfaction; but this satisfaction does by no means diminish my oppression or my pain. Nor could there possibly befall me a pain so great, that it could move me to swerve from the divine ordination, or leave my prison, or wish to leave it until God is satisfied, nor could I experience any woe so great as would be an escape from his divine decree, so merciful and so full of justice do I find it.

"I see these things clearly, but words fail me to describe them as I wish. What I have described is going on within my spirit, and therefore I have said it. The prison which detains me is the world; my chains, the body; the soul, illuminated by grace, comprehends how great a misery it is to be hindered from her final end, and she suffers greatly because she is very tender. She receives from God, by his grace, a certain dignity which assimilates her to him, nay, which makes her one with him by the participation of his goodness. And as it is impossible for God to suffer any pain, it is so also with those happy souls who are drawing nearer to him. The more closely they approach him the more fully do they share in his perfections.

"Any delay, then, causes the soul intolerable pain. The pain and the delay prevent the full action both of what is hers by nature, and of that which has been revealed to her by grace; and, not able as yet to possess and still essentially capable of possessing, her pain is great in proportion to her desire of God. The more perfectly she knows him, the more ardent is her desire, and the more sinless is she. The impediments that bar her from him become all the more terrible to her, because she is so wholly bent on him, and when not one of these is left she knows him as he is.

"As a man who suffers death rather than offend God does not become insensible to the pains of death, but is so illuminated by God that his zeal for the divine honor is greater than his love for life, so the soul, knowing the will of God, esteems it more than all outward or inward torments, however terrible; and this for the reason that God, for whom and by whom the work is done, is infinitely more desirable than all else that can be known or understood. And inasmuch as God keeps the soul absorbed in himself and in his majesty, even though it be only in a slight degree, yet she can attach no importance to anything beside. She loses in him all that is her own, and can neither see nor speak, nor yet be conscious of any injury or pain she suffers, but as I have said before it is all understood in one moment as she passes from this life. And finally, to conclude all, understand well, that in the almighty and merciful God, all that is in man is wholly transformed, and that purgatory purifies him."

THE END

Also from Benediction Books ...
Wandering Between Two Worlds: Essays on Faith and Art
Anita Mathias
Benediction Books, 2007
152 pages
ISBN: 0955373700

Available from www.amazon.com, www.amazon.co.uk

In these wide-ranging lyrical essays, Anita Mathias writes, in lush, lovely prose, of her naughty Catholic childhood in Jamshedpur, India; her large, eccentric family in Mangalore, a seacoast town converted by the Portuguese in the sixteenth century; her rebellion and atheism as a teenager in her Himalayan boarding school, run by German missionary nuns, St. Mary's Convent, Nainital; and her abrupt religious conversion after which she entered Mother Teresa's convent in Calcutta as a novice. Later rich, elegant essays explore the dualities of her life as a writer, mother, and Christian in the United States-- Domesticity and Art, Writing and Prayer, and the experience of being "an alien and stranger" as an immigrant in America, sensing the need for roots.

About the Author

Anita Mathias is the author of *Wandering Between Two Worlds: Essays on Faith and Art.* She has a B.A. and M.A. in English from Somerville College, Oxford University, and an M.A. in Creative Writing from the Ohio State University, USA. Anita won a National Endowment of the Arts fellowship in Creative Nonfiction in 1997. She lives in Oxford, England with her husband, Roy, and her daughters, Zoe and Irene.

Visit Anita's website
http://www.anitamathias.com,
and Anita's blog
http://dreamingbeneaththespires.blogspot.com (Dreaming Beneath the Spires).

.

The Church That Had Too Much
Anita Mathias
Benediction Books, 2010
52 pages
ISBN: 9781849026567

Available from www.amazon.com, www.amazon.co.uk

The Church That Had Too Much was very well-intentioned. She wanted to love God, she wanted to love people, but she was both hampered by her muchness and the abundance of her posses-sions, and beset by ambition, power struggles and snobbery. Read about the surprising way The Church That Had Too Much began to resolve her problems in this deceptively simple and en-chanting fable.

About the Author

Anita Mathias is the author of *Wandering Between Two Worlds: Essays on Faith and Art.* She has a B.A. and M.A. in English from Somerville College, Oxford University, and an M.A. in Creative Writing from the Ohio State University, USA. Anita won a National Endowment of the Arts fellowship in Creative Nonfiction in 1997. She lives in Oxford, England with her hus-band, Roy, and her daughters, Zoe and Irene.

Visit Anita's website
  http://www.anitamathias.com,
and Anita's blog
  http://dreamingbeneaththespires.blogspot.com (Dreaming Beneath the Spires).